ANTIQ

A to Z

a pocket handbook for collectors and dealers by

EDWARD WENHAM

formerly Editor of the Connoisseur
with sections on Weapons
and Armour by 'SEGALAS'

London: G. BELL & SONS, LTD

Clocks

Enamels

Furniture

Furniture Woods

Veneers, Marquetry
and Inlay

Glass

Pewter, Copper
and Brass

Pottery and
Porcelain

Sheffield Plate

Silver

Firearms

Edged Weapons

Armour

CONTENTS

BAROMETERS *

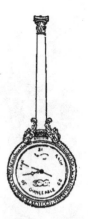

AELLOSCOPE. Name given to an instrument invented and patented in 1861 by an American, H. A. Clum. In *Wonderful Inventions* (1882), it is described as, 'An apparatus . . . named because its special function is the viewing or indicating of storms. It combines the construction of a barometer, having a cistern containing 70 lb. of mercury and a central mercurial column 2¼ inches in diameter. In this column rests a float or buoy supporting large cylinders or air chambers. . . .' It was claimed that these cylinders were so sensitive to atmospheric changes that they showed variations not observable in the ordinary barometer.

ANEROID BAROMETER. This type of barometer is said to have been invented by a Frenchman, Lucien Vidie, about 1845. The principle of the instrument, described briefly, is the weight of a column of air which, in a common barometer, acts on the mercury in the aneroid, presses on a small metal box from which nearly all the air is extracted,

and the hand or pointer is connected to this box by delicately adjusted mechanism; when the atmospheric pressure on the vacuum box is lessened, a spring acting on levers turns the hand to the left; when the pressure increases, the spring causes the hand to turn to the right.

BANJO SHAPE. The style of case similar to the outline of a banjo used with the wheel barometer of the later 18th century and after. It was widely popular and large numbers still exist in perfect working order. *See* illustration above.

BAROGRAPH. An automatic instrument with which an ink-fed style (pen) registers the varying atmospheric pressures on paper stretched round a drum—in other words a self-recording barometer.

BAROMETER, ORIGIN OF. The discovery of the barometer was the outcome of a young Italian's refusing to accept the doctrine that nature abhors a vacuum. In the early 17th century, some Italian

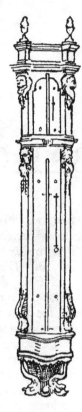

Late Georgian barometer ornamented in the Adam manner

Late Georgian barometer with a small clock

Georgian mural barometer in Chippendale carved case

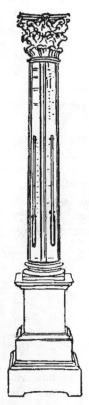

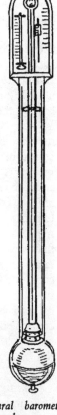

Table barometer in the form of a Corinthian column. c. 1805

Mirror in wide, lacquered frame with diagonal barometer and thermometer. Early 18th century

Mural barometer in mahogany case. New York, c. 1810

pump-makers found that water could not be raised to a greater height than about 32 feet by a suction pump. They consulted Galileo, the famous astrologer, who pacified them by explaining nature's abhorence of a vacuum and then set his pupil Torricelli the task of finding the real solution. Torricelli felt he could explain the phenomenon if he could prove the atmosphere had weight and that the weight would exercise a pressure equal to a column of water 32 feet high. To test this, he decided to use mercury in place of water, as, mercury being 13½ times heavier than water would allow an experiment on a much smaller scale. He contended that if the atmosphere was the counterpoise to a 32 feet column of water, then it should counterpoise a column of approximately 28 inches of mercury and this was the basis of his experiment.

Taking a tube about 36 inches long and ¼ inch inside diameter, he sealed one end and filled the tube with mercury. Stopping the open end with a finger, he inverted the tube, placing the open end in a vessel containing mercury, removing the finger, but holding the tube in a vertical position. The mercury in the tube sank immediately to about 28 inches above the level of the mercury in the vessel, leaving in the upper part of the tube an empty space which came to be called the Torricellian vacuum. This proved that the top of the column was free from atmospheric pressure, but the weight of the mercury remaining

in the tube was supported by the pressure of the atmosphere on that in the open vessel in which the tube was standing. Torricelli died before he had completed his discovery, for while he knew that some influence acted as a counterpoise to the mercury, he had not yet proved it was the atmosphere.

BAROSCOPE. A device which shows, approximately, the variations in the atmospheric pressure without measurements; for example, a bottle of liquid with some object in suspension which rises and falls with the changes in the atmosphere. *See* WEATHER GLASS.

BOURDON BAROMETER. *See* MANOMETER.

CISTERN BAROMETER. Based upon Torricelli's experiment, but to make a more easily portable barometer, the reservoir or cistern holding the mercury, in which the open end of the tube was placed, was covered in, a tiny hole being made to let in the air; with this type the tube was usually fixed to a wood frame, on the upper part of which there was a scale and movable pointer showing the level of the mercury on the scale. With a barometer of this kind, the scale does not always show the true height of the column (i.e. the mercury in the tube) above the surface of that in the cistern which, of necessity, rises as that in the tube sinks. *See* FORTIN'S BAROMETER.

CORRECT POSITION. A barometer, whether of the hanging or standing kind, must be perpendicular, because the perpendicular distance between the surface of the mercury in the cistern and the top of that in the tube is the real height of the barometer.

DESCARTES, RENÉ. A French philosopher who is said to have made the same observation as Torricelli twelve years before the latter made his experiment.

DIAGONAL BAROMETER. Often called the yard-arm, the diagonal barometer is usually mounted on a wide wood frame which holds a mirror or a perpetual calendar. One section of the tube rises vertically from the cistern and, at the angle of the frame, continues diagonally across the top. The diagonal section is fitted on a plate engraved with the scale and the words Variable, Fair, etc., denoting the weather, while a thermometer with its appropriate scale is fixed to the other vertical side of the frame.

ELEVATION. After Torricelli died in 1647, the suggestion that the weight of air was the counterpoise of the mercury (see BAROMETER) was taken up by others both in France and England. Upon this assumption it was contended that at higher altitudes the pressure of air perforce would decrease and consequently the column of mercury would be proportionately lower. The barometer was read at different altitudes on Puy de Dôme mountain and it was found that the mercury was three inches higher at the base than at the summit which was three thousand feet above sea level. It was also discovered that the height of the mercury varied when stationary and that these variations were coincidental with or were followed by meteorological changes, and so the barometer became the instrument for predicting the weather. It was also realized that the height of the mercury column varies with the altitude at which it was read, conversely a barometer was a means for measuring altitudes.

FORTIN'S BAROMETER. The source of error with the cistern barometer (q.v.) was overcome in Fortin's barometer. With this the cistern is cylindrical, the upper part being glass while the base is of flexible leather which is raised or lowered by a screw. By this device, the level of the mercury can be kept constant; also, when travelling, the cistern may be filled completely by screwing up the leather base so avoiding the risk of air bubbles or of the weight of the mercury breaking the tube when being moved.

HANGING BAROMETER. See PORTABLE BAROMETER.

HUYGENS' BAROMETER. Christian Huygens, the Dutch astronomer, adopted a barometer tube expanded at the top to a cylindrical shape in which a fine tube, partly filled with water, was placed; by this means, changes in the barometer pressure were more easily seen because a small change in the level of the mercury caused a larger variation of the water; but as with other water barometers this method failed.

MANOMETER. Vidie patented his device for the aneroid barometer (q.v.) in 1845, but aneroids were not made commercially until about

1849 when Eugene Bourdon invented and patented his metallic manometer (an instrument for measuring the rarety of the atmosphere, gases, and vapours) known as the Bourdon Gauge one end of which carries the registering pointer. Vidie brought an action for infringement against Bourdon who had to stop making his barometer.

MERCURIAL BAROMETER. The more common type consisting of a tube about 36 inches long containing mercury and closed at the upper end.

PENDENT BAROMETER. A funnel-shaped tube closed at the smaller end and hung vertically with the large end downward. The length of the column of mercury in the tube adjusted itself to the atmospheric pressure exercised at the wide open end. Unfortunately the slightest jar caused the mercury to fall from the tube, so this late 17th-century invention passed to forgotten things.

PORTABLE BAROMETER. Two kinds of portable barometers were developed from the original cistern type during the late 17th century and after, i.e. one for standing on the table and one for hanging on the wall. The former were usually in the form of a turned pillar, in which the tube of mercury was enclosed, and a scale at the top of the pillar which is usually fitted with four hinged metal feet. Daniel Quare, the famous 17th-century clockmaker, patented a device which was similar to that used by Fortin (q.v.). This was a pad fitted at the bottom of the tube of mercury; the pad was attached to a threaded rod which passed through the cistern at the base of the pillar with a knob at the other end of the rod. By turning the barometer upside down, the tube filled with mercury when the rod was screwed up and the pad sealed the tube so that the barometer could be carried.

SIGN POST. See DIAGONAL.

SIPHON BAROMETER. A J-shaped tube with one leg much longer than the other. The longer leg is filled with mercury and closed at the end and the shorter one which acts as a cistern is left open. The difference between the levels of the mercury in the two legs being the height of the barometer. The siphon was adapted to the wheel barometer (q.v.).

SYMPIEZOMETER. A glass tube expanded at the top with an open cistern at the bottom end. The lower tube and cistern contained liquid such as oil or glycerine and the upper part an elastic gas. As the atmospheric pressure increased the liquid rose and the gas was compressed, when it lessened the liquid fell and the gas expanded. A sensitive barometer but not strictly accurate. It has long since been superseded by the aneroid.

VERNIER. A short movable scale made to slide along the divisions of a graduated instrument to obtain fractional parts of the sub-divisions, for example a barometer scale.

WEATHER GLASS. Various types of simple weather foretellers, which are really baroscopes, were formerly used in cottage homes. One was a half section of a glass pear shape with a long tubular spout protruding from the lower part of the bulbous section, the flat side hanging against the wall. The container which was sealed at the top is filled with water and the atmospheric pressure is indicated by the level of the water in the spout.

WHEEL BAROMETER. Dr. Robert Hooke invented the wheel barometer which is merely a siphon type (q.v.), a weight, float and a small wheel to which a pointer is fixed. The banjo-shaped 'weather glass' still familiar in modern homes is a descendant of Hooke's invention. The J-shaped siphon tube containing the mercury is fixed to the inside of the case; at the back of the dial there is a small pulley wheel with the indicator fastened to the end of the spindle extending through the dial. A short length of thread with a glass float at one end and a small glass weight at the other passes round the pulley. The float rests on the surface of the mercury in the short leg of the J-shaped siphon, and the small glass weight which is slightly lighter than the float is suspended in a short length of tube to ensure its moving freely. As the atmospheric pressure changes the level of the mercury, the float falls or rises, thus changing the level of the float, causing the pulley to turn to the left or right and so move the pointer on the scale engraved on the dial. If the mercury falls, the needle moves to *Rain, Much Rain,* etc., and, if it rises, to *Fair, Set Fair,* etc. The wheel barometer did not come into fashionable use until the second half of the 18th century.

YARD-ARM BAROMETER. *See* DIAGONAL BAROMETER.

BIBLIOGRAPHY

SCIENCE MUSEUM: *Catalogue of the Meteorological Collections.* 1922.

TIMBS, JOHN: *Wonderful Inventions.* 1882.

MACQUOID, PERCY and EDWARDS, RALPH: *The Dictionary of English Furniture from the Middle Ages to the Late Georgian Period.* 1924-27. 3 vols.

13

CLOCKS ✫

ACT OF PARLIAMENT CLOCK. Large circular or octagonal wood dial painted black with hour figures in gilt and a long rectangular or shaped trunk. They were installed in post-houses and inns when tax was imposed on all kinds of timepieces in 1797 and people refused to buy watches or clocks and disposed of any they owned.

ALARUM. The mechanism of a clock controlling a bell which could be set to sound at a particular time, i.e. an alarm.

ANCHOR ESCAPEMENT. Recoil escapement with two anchor-shaped arms each with an inclined pallet which engages the escape wheel. One of the most generally used escapements for clocks. Invented about 1670-75.

ARBOR. Axle or spindle of a wheel in a clock or watch.

ASTRONOMICAL CLOCK. Clock showing on separate dials, the date, day of the week, phases of the moon and other astronomical data.

BACK PLATE. Engraved brass plate at back of a bracket clock.

BALANCE. A vibrating cross-bar with weights (FOLIOT) used with a verge escapement, later superseded by a vibrating wheel having a semi-rotary action.

BANJO CLOCK. An eight-day weight-driven clock, adapted in 1802, by Simon Willard of Roxbury, Massachusetts from an English wall clock. The name derives from the case which has a circular head, narrow body sloping slightly to a rectangular box-like base with a flat bottom or an applied ornament. The earlier clocks of this type are timepieces only, but some of the later ones have a striking movement with a bell at the top of the case.

BARREL. Drum-like cylinder on which the line carrying a clock weight is wound or which contains the mainspring.

BEDPOST CLOCK. One of the names applied to a lantern clock.

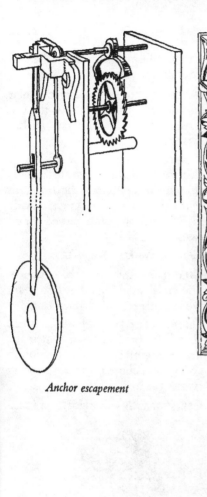

Anchor escapement

Back plate

Balance wheel

Banjo clock

Candle clock

BIRDCAGE CLOCK. One of the names applied to a lantern clock.

BRACKET CLOCK CASES

Arch top. Case with straight sides and semi-circular top.

Balloon. Top rounded as with arch top but lower part of case incurved or waisted.

Basket top. An early case with domical oblong top formed of four sections of quarter round mitred. Also with applied metal ornaments or entirely of pierced and chased metal.

Bell top. Case surmounted by an ornamental shape with concave sides and a small domed top.

Broken arch. Case with rounded arch top, but the arch instead of extending the full width of the case, is 'broken' and finishes on each side with a flat moulded section.

Double basket top. Case with intricately pierced and chased metal top consisting of two sections.

Lancet. Similar to the arch top case, but with a pointed arch, resembling the lancet windows of Gothic architecture.

BULL'S EYE. A small round or oval piece of glass fitted in the door of a grandfather clock case. *See* GLASS section.

CANDLE CLOCK. A glass dial fitted to a tubular candlestick containing a spring for raising the candle as it burns; the heat from the flame turns a small fly-wheel which operates the hands. A clock for use at night.

CANDLE DIAL. Candle in a candlestick fitted with a bracket supporting a gnomon (bar to cast a shadow) and a card marked with the hours; as the candle burns down, the shadow from the gnomon shows the hour.

CARRIAGE CLOCK. Small rectangular case of brass with handle at the top often fitted in additional leather case for travelling.

CARTEL CLOCK. Wall clock in elaborate gilded bronze case fashionable in France during the late 17th century. Similar clocks were made in England but with carved wood cases.

CENTRE WHEEL. *See* WHEELS.

CHAPTER. Any of the Roman numerals marking the hours on what is called the chapter ring.

CHOPS. The two sides of a small, cleft brass bracket from which the flat suspension spring of a pendulum swings; the chops prevent the spring twisting. *See* COCK.

CLEPSYDRA. A water clock; any con-

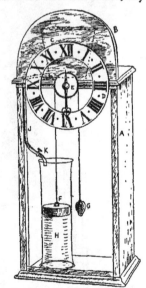

trivance by which time is measured by a regulated flow of water.

CLICK. A catch or stop made to fall into the teeth of a wheel and so allow it to move only in one direction.

CLOCK. The word is derived from the Old English *clokke* and the Old French, *cloque*, meaning a bell; in early days the hour shown on the sundial was marked by sounding a bell.

COACH CLOCK. Portable timepiece similar to but much larger than modern watches—some were 7 inches diameter; used when travelling until railways replaced coaches.

COCK. The projecting bracket at the back supporting the pendulum of a clock. *See* JAWS.

COCK ORNAMENT. Ornament fixed to the back plate of a bracket clock to conceal the pendulum suspension. Similarly elaborate designs are found with early watches; to-day, these are joined to form a bracelet or other personal adornment.

CONGREVE CLOCK. A pivoted sloping plate on which a small steel ball runs in channels down the incline; at the lowest point the ball strikes a release, the plate changes its incline to the opposite direction when the ball returns along the channels and repeats the release on the other side. Invented by William Congreve in 1808.

CORNER ORNAMENTS. *See* SPANDREL ORNAMENTS.

CONTRATE WHEEL. *See* WHEELS.

CROMWELLIAN CLOCK. A name sometimes applied to a lantern clock.

CROWN WHEEL. *See* WHEELS.

CRUTCH. A light steel rod fixed to the arbor of the anchor (pallet arbor) with an arm in the form of a pin, a loop or a fork at a right angle with the lower end; the pin passes through and rides in a slot in a flat pendulum rod or the latter passes through the loop or rides in the fork.

CURSOR. Sliding ring drilled with small hole and fitted to a ring dial (q.v.) for adjusting to the latitude and season.

CYCLOIDAL CHEEKS. Two curved

pieces of flexible steel, between which Christian Huygens suspended the pendulum by two cords with the first pendulum clock, to ensure the time occupied by the swing was unaffected by the arc or distance the pendulum travelled. The cheeks were later replaced by the suspension spring.

DRIVING WHEEL. *See* WHEELS.

EQUATION DIAL. A subsidiary dial with a scale marked *Sun Slower* on the left and *Sun Faster* on the right, indicating the difference between mean time and sun time.

EQUATION OF TIME. The difference between apparent time shown by the real sun and that reckoned by the imaginary 'mean' sun, adopted to overcome the slight variation in the sun's movement. Apparent or true sun noon ranges, at different times of the year, from 16 minutes 19 seconds in November *before* to 14 minutes 25 seconds in February *after* Greenwich mean time.

ESCAPEMENT. A device connecting the train of wheels of a clock and giving impulse to the balance or pendulum and controlling the outlet or 'escape' of the driving power.

ESCAPE WHEEL. *See* WHEELS.

FALLING BALL CLOCK. A brass sphere or ball with a band round the middle marked with the hours in two series of I to XII. The cord, passing through the sphere, was wound round a barrel and the weight of the movement and ball pulling downward supplied the power to operate the movement. The hour band revolved and the time was indicated by a pointer. When the ball had dropped to the full length of the cord, it was raised slowly by hand and the cord re-wound itself on the barrel.

FAN FLY. A small fan-like device connected with a striking train to regulate the speed.

FIRST WHEEL. *See* WHEELS.

FLEUR DE LIS. *See* HAND.

FOLIOT. Cross-bar with adjustable weights serving as a regulator with a verge escapement.

FRETS. Pierced ornaments fitted to the top of the front and sides of a lantern clock.

FUSEE. A spirally grooved conical pulley from which a gut or chain is unwound on to a barrel containing the spring; invented by Jacob Zech of Prague about 1525.

GATHERING PALLET. Small rotating tooth that 'pulls back' the rack (q.v.) of the striking mechanism. *See* illustration, p. 21.

GNOMON. Style, pin or vertical plate casting shadow on face of sun-dial.

HALIFAX CLOCK. Grandfather clock with rotating globular moon over the dial.

HAND. The pointer of early clocks was the shape of a hand with the index finger extended—hence the term 'hand'.

HEMICYCLE. A half-basin shape cut from a block of stone, the inside surface divided into twelve parts of the day, radiating from the gnomon (q.v.) the shadow of which indicated the hour.

HOROLOGE. An instrument which indicates the time of day.

HOUR. Derived from Greek *hora* (a season) adopted during second century B.C. to denote the twenty-fourth part of a day.

HOUR GLASS. *See* SAND GLASS.

HOUR WHEEL. *See* WHEELS.

JACK. Mechanical figure, usually of a man, which strikes the time on a bell connected with ancient clocks.

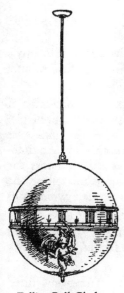

Falling Ball Clock

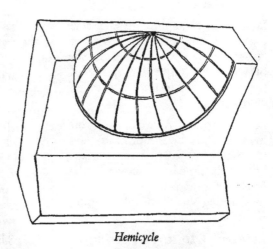

Hemicycle

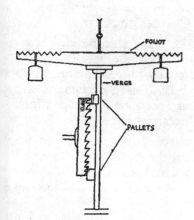

FOLIOT

VERGE

PALLETS

Verge and Foliot

Fret

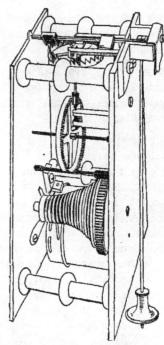

Movement with spring and fusee drive, horizontal crown wheel and short pendulum

JAWS. Term applied to the side pieces of the projecting bracket known as the cock (q.v.) in the slit of which the suspension spring of the pendulum is placed; also called chops (q.v.).

LAMP CLOCK. A glass reservoir marked with hour numerals, and containing oil fed to a small wick-holder, the time being shown by the level of the oil as it is consumed by the burning wick. *See* illustration, p. 14.

LANTERN CLOCK. Weight-driven striking timepiece with verge escapement in brass case, large bell above ornamented with frets (q.v.).

LEAVES. *See* PINION.

LEVER ESCAPEMENT. Invented by Thomas Mudge, about 1760, but not generally adopted until much later.

LIFTING PIECE. An L-shaped part which raises the rack-hook and releases the rack-striking mechanism. *See* illustration, p. 21.

LOCKING-PLATE. A plate with notches at varying intervals round the edge, also called a count-wheel. It controlled the number of strikes made by the hammer on the bell. For example, at one o'clock a tooth falls into a notch after the bell has sounded once; for two o'clock the wheel turns a slightly longer distance before the notch is reached and so on for each successive hour. The locking-plate was superseded by the rack and snail (q.v.).

MEAN TIME. Time as reckoned by an imaginary or 'mean' sun which moves in the equator at a uniform

speed based upon the average rate of the real sun.

MINUTE. Derived from Ptolemy's *partes minutae primae*—first minute divisions. *See* SECOND.

MUSICAL CLOCK. An adaptation of the early musical box principle. The cylinder with the pins was applied to the mechanism of a timepiece so that at certain hours the various pins tripped the tail of one of a series of hammers which falls on its own particular bell.

NEF. Silver model of an ancient ship called a nef fitted with a clock movement.

NIGHT CLOCKS. Timepieces fitted with a dial lighted, usually from behind, by a candle or night-light. *See* CANDLE CLOCK.

PALLET. A detent or click connected with the vibrating piece transmitting successive impulses to the balance or pendulum; it also acts as a check on the escape wheel. *See* ESCAPEMENT.

PENDULUM. A weight, called the bob, at the end of a rod suspended by a flexible spring, which swings freely and regulates a clock movement.

PINION. A cog wheel with a small number of teeth, called leaves, geared with a larger wheel.

PIN WHEEL. *See* WHEELS.

PIPE. A hollow socket carrying the hour hand. *See* HOUR WHEEL.

RACK. The part of the rack-striking mechanism controlling the number of strokes of the hammer on the gong. *See* illustration, p. 21.

Lantern clock

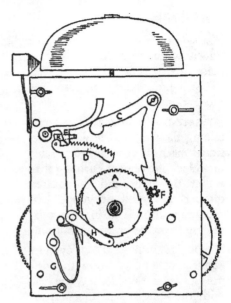

Motion work of an 8-day clock. A, large wheel with 72 teeth. B, Snail, which controls the striking. C, lifting piece. D, rack. E, rack hook or click. F, motion or reversed wheel. G, spring. H, tail at bottom of rack. J, deepest part of snail. K, gathering pallet

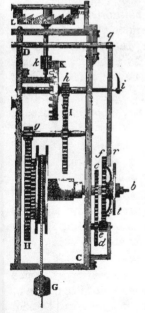

Pinions at e, g, h, k

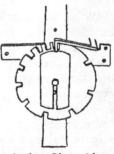

Locking Plate with arm hook

21

RACK-HOOK. A tooth or click which when raised by the lifting piece (q.v.) releases the rack to set the striking train in motion. *See* illustration, p. 21.

REPEATING MOVEMENT. For ascertaining the time in the dark, additional mechanism was incorporated in a clock movement enabling it to repeat the hour and the nearest quarter on a bell or gong. The repeating action is set in motion by pulling a cord or pressing a button.

RING DIAL. A shallow cylinder about 2 inches diameter with a tiny hole drilled in the side. When held with the hole toward the sun, the rays passed through, throwing a spot of light on hour numerals on the inside surface. *See* CURSOR.

ROLLING CLOCK. Small movement in circular metal case marked with hours on the side. It was placed on a smooth slanting board down which it rolled very slowly, thus setting the train in motion. The time was indicated by a pointer which retained an upright position, pointing the time as the hours on the dial rolled by. Invented about 1661 by Edward Somerset, Marquis of Worcester.

SAND GLASS. Two pear-shaped glass bulbs joined at the small ends and fitted in a frame; the upper bulb contains a quantity of sand which, in a fixed period of time, runs through a small opening to the lower bulb—one hour, half an hour or other periods according to the size of the bulbs and the amount of sand. Time was kept in the Royal Navy by hour and half-hour sand-glasses until the early years of Queen Victoria's reign.

SCRATCH DIAL. Miniature sundials at one time scratched on the south wall of country churches, barns and other buildings.

SECOND. Derived from Ptolemy's *partes minutae secundae*—second minute divisions.

SHEEPS-HEAD CLOCK. Name given to lantern clocks when the dial projects to an unusual extent on each side.

SNAIL. A stepped plate similar to the shape of a snail, moving with the hour hand and regulating the number of strokes on the bell at each hour. *See* illustration, p. 21.

SOLAR or SUN TIME. Time of day reckoned by diurnal motion of the true sun. When the sun is at its greatest height, i.e. when the shadow is the shortest, it is twelve o'clock true noon which varies from 16 minutes 19 seconds *before* to 14 minutes 25 seconds *after* Greenwich 'mean' noon. *See* MEAN TIME.

SPADE HAND. An early clock hand somewhat resembling the ace of spades.

SPANDREL. The space formed by the arch of the hour ring and the angle of the dial plate.

SPANDREL ORNAMENT. Introduced about 1670 when a simple winged cherub was used; later the spandrel or corner ornaments were larger and more elaborate.

SPRING. The mainspring is believed to be the invention of Peter Hele of Nuremberg in the early 16th century.

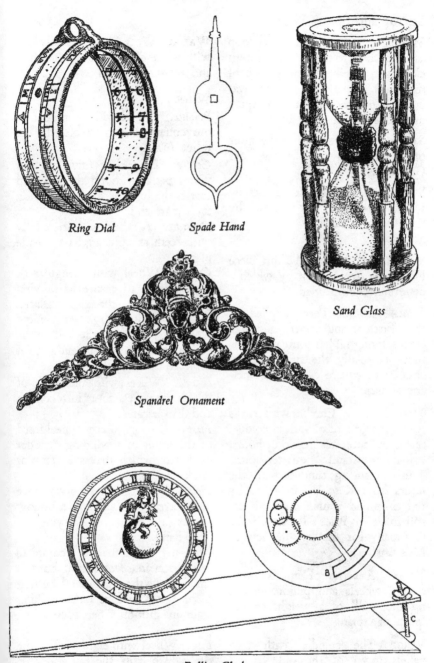

Ring Dial

Spade Hand

Sand Glass

Spandrel Ornament

Rolling Clock

A, hemispherical centre loaded with lead to keep pointer upright.   B, stout arm
with weight.   C, screw to adjust speed

STIRRUP AND SPUR. A metal loop (stirrup) fixed to the top of a lantern clock and a spike (spur) to each of the back legs. The stirrup was fastened to the wall and the spurs driven firmly into the wall.

STYLE. A pin indicating the hour on a sundial by its shadow. *See* GNOMON.

SUNDIAL. A plate with a dial on which the time of day is shown by the shadow cast by a style or gnomon.

SUSPENSION SPRING. A short piece of flexible steel ribbon by which a pendulum is suspended.

TABLE CLOCK. Term applied to the first spring-driven portable clocks, though it has come to denote more especially the timepieces in circular or square cases with horizontal dials.

TIME CANDLES. Candles with marks round the sides or of various colours at regular intervals denoting hours, half-hours and quarter-hours. Time-measuring candles with the hours from X to VII indicated by red rings and roman numerals are still made by Price's Patent Candle Company for use by the Science Museum.

TRAIN. A series of interworking geared wheels and pinions driven by the 'pull' of a weight or the 'push' of a spring.

VERGE. The spindle with two pallets (q.v.) of the old vertical escapement known as the verge— the first form of recoil escapement. From verge, a staff or rod.

WAG-ON-WALL CLOCK. Wall clock with white dial, the long pendulum and weights exposed.

WHEELS

Balance. Wheel with a semi-rotary movement which replaced the foliot (q.v.).

Centre. The arbor (q.v.) of this wheel passes through the dial and carries the long or minute hand on the square end.

Contrate. A wheel set horizontally with teeth at right angles with the plane.

Crown. Wheel with triangular or ratchet teeth to ensure its moving only in one direction. Placed vertically with verge escapement where its progress is checked by the pallets; with the short pendulum it is placed horizontally.

Escape. Wheel with the teeth of which the pallets come into contact and then 'escape'.

First or *Driving.* Large wheel fixed to the arbor of a winding cylinder or barrel which drives a train of wheels and pinions.

Hour. Wheel that revolves once in twelve hours and has a hollow socket or 'pipe' (q.v.) carrying the hour hand.

Motion. Wheel making a complete revolution in reverse each hour, a small pin on the side raises the lifting piece (q.v.) and sets the striking train in motion. *See* illustration, p. 21.

Pin. Wheel with eight pins on the rim which 'trip' the tail and raise the striking hammer.

Second. Wheel driven by the centre wheel through a pinion on its arbor.

BIBLIOGRAPHY

Britten, F. J.: *Old Clocks and Watches and their Makers.* 6th ed. 1932.

Britten, F. W.: *Horological Hints and Helps.* 1934.

Cescinsky, H.: *Old English Master Clockmakers and their Clocks.* 1938.

Cescinsky, H. and Webster, M. R.: *English Domestic Clocks.* 1913.

Eden, H. K. E. and Lloyd, E.: *The Book of Sundials.* 1900.

Encyclopaedia Britannica: Articles on Clocks, Dials and Equation of Time.

Reid, Thomas: *Clock and Watch Making.* 1846.

Timbs, John: *Wonderful Inventions.* 1882.

Ward, F. A. B.: *Handbook of the Collections Illustrating Time Measurement: Science Museum.*

Wenham, Edward: *Old Clocks for Modern Use.* 1951.

WHEELS
(*see opposite*)

1. *First or Driving Wheel*

2. *Barrel*

3. *Centre Pinion*

4. *Centre Wheel*

5. *Pinion of Second Wheel*

6. *Second Wheel*

7. *Pinion of Escape Whee*

8. *Escape Wheel*

9. *Pallets*

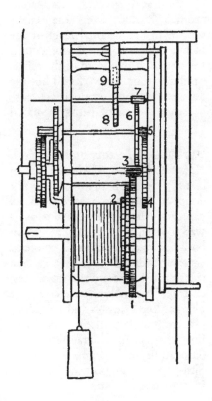

ENAMELS ✷

GEN. CLINTON

BASSE TAILLE. A process in which the design is carved in low relief in the metal ground, transparent enamel floated over the entire surface to the original level of the metal, the strength of any colour varying with the depth of the relief; similar to Champlevé (q.v.) but the different coloured enamels are close together instead of being separated by metal strips.

BATTERSEA. Factory started at York House by Stephen Theodore Janssen in 1753 closed in 1756. The work done at Battersea was on-enamel painting, namely, the metal ground was covered with white enamel on both sides and decoration in coloured enamels painted over it. Printed transfer designs were also used. The characteristic colours are a bright blue, a deep crimson and a reddish-brown, the last often being used for the printed transfers. The decoration was figures, flowers, birds, landscapes, portraits of prominent characters, etc.

BILSTON. *See* STAFFORDSHIRE ENAMELS.

CANTON. Painted enamels on metal were introduced from Europe to China where they are generally known as *Yang Tz'u* meaning literally foreign porcelain. Limoges enamels were sent to China and copied; they have come to be called Canton enamels because that city is the principal centre where the work is made.

CHAMPLEVÉ. With this process of enamelling, the cells or troughs are cut out of heavy copper so as to leave metal lines or partitions raised between the cells and forming the outline of the design. Powdered enamel was placed in the cells and fused after which it was smoothed and polished.

CLOISONNÉ. Thin metal strips bent to the outline of the design and fastened to the copper ground—the strips being raised from troughs or cells on which powdered enamel is placed and fused as with Champlevé (q.v.).

CLOISONS. Divisions or partitions, i.e. the metal strips forming the parts in cloisonné; sometimes called 'tapes'.

COLOURS. Enamel is glass, so it is coloured by metallic oxides; the actual colour is determined by the character of the glass, the nature of the oxide, and the amount of heat to which it is subjected. Thus copper can give emerald green, deep red or with a soda base, turquoise blue; manganese gives purple; gold, a pale rosy red; silver, a clear yellow; iron, a coral red or sea green or brownish-yellow; chromium, an opaque green; cobalt, various blues except turquoise; antimonate of lead, an opaque yellow.

ENAMEL. A deposit of a vitreous compound in the form of glass applied to a metal surface as powder or paste (q.v.) and fused upon the metal in a kiln or under a blow-pipe.

FIRE-POLISHED. When enamel is left untouched instead of being ground after it is taken from the kiln, it is called 'fire polished'; this treatment gives an added beauty as it results in the surface being slightly convex.

FIRING. Owing to the differences in the nature of the various oxides, enamel colours demand different degrees of heat to fuse them. Those which withstand the greatest heat are fired first, then those which withstand less and so on to gold ruby which can be subjected to a relatively slight fire.

GRISAILLE. Enamel painting in grisaille appeared about 1525. The copper was covered with black and fired; the black then being modified to a dark grey by a very thin coating of white. Before this was fired the outline of a design was sketched on, and the outline scratched out down to the black. Then the coating of white was removed from the parts intended for the background and from any parts which were to show the full black. After this was fixed, the artist finished the picture by painting in white; where darker shading was needed, the white was laid on thinly, and for the lighter parts more heavily—with the latter, the white enamel was 'built up' gradually by successive paintings, each of which was fired.

LIMOGES. The name of this French city has been closely associated with enamelling since medieval times, the earliest examples being ascribed to the end of the 12th century. During the following hundred years, large quantities of enamel work were made at Limoges—'good, indifferent and downright bad' as one writer expresses it. In fact, the quality declined to such an extent by the 14th century, it lost its popularity. Some of the Limoges champlevé lines were punched with a small pattern which suggests a twisted or milled wire. After being the centre of the art in medieval times, it was the source of its revival and again the centre; and this revival saw the introduction of a variation of the *basse taille* process (q.v.). Instead of modelling figures, lines were engraved in the shallow colour cells or troughs and blackened, the troughs then being filled with translucent enamel—later the black lines were painted in. That was the early method of drawing the outline and filling it with translucent enamel, later perfected by Nardon Penicaud.

PASTE. Enamel colour is virtually coloured glass ground to powder and made into what is known as a 'paste' which when dry is placed on the metal ground and fused (melted).

PLIQUE-À-JOUR. Similar to the cloisonné except that the troughs or cells have no bottom; the light therefore shows through the translucent enamels which thus resemble miniature stained glass.

SCRATCHING OUT LINES. While the paste was of the right consistency, lines were scratched in it and filled with paste or powder of a different colour to obtain shading effects.

STAFFORDSHIRE PAINTED ENAMELS. On-enamel painting similar to that of Battersea (q.v.) was produced at Bilston and Wednesbury in Staffordshire; but the work of the Staffordshire artists is distinguished by the beautiful ground colours— a deep rich blue; turquoise; light green; maroon; yellow; lavender; various reds and some others. Bilston and Wednesbury enamel work shows clearly that efforts were made to imitate the French models. Of the men working at Bilston during the later 18th century, John Green, Henry Beckett, Benjamin Bickley were prominent.

TAPES OF METAL. *See* CLOISONS.

Battersea Enamel box with a gilt-metal mount, the lid painted with bouquet of flowers in colours

Battersea Enamel box formed as a shoe, painted with flower sprays on a white ground

At the head of this section is an oval plaque transfer printed in sepia with a portrait and in a metal frame

BIBLIOGRAPHY

CUNYNGHAME, H.: *Art of Enamelling on Metals.* 1906.
DALPAYRAT, L.: *Limoges Enamels.*
MEW, EGAN: *Battersea Enamels, selected and described.* 1926.

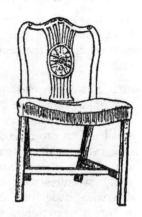

FURNITURE ✶

ABASCUS. The member or section of an architectural capital immediately below the architrave (q.v.).

ACANTHUS. A conventionalized

form of the acanthus leaf used in Greek architecture adapted as an ornament with furniture and silver.

ACORN TURNING. Turned shapes in the form of an acorn used with early 17th-century chairs.

ADAM STYLE. Formal designs of the late 18th century by the brothers Adam based on the classic art discovered at Pompeii and Herculaneum. Chair and table legs, tapering round or square and often fluted. Typical ornaments were paterae, winged sphinx, swags, Vitruvian scroll, Greek fret, anthemion, goats' and lions' heads.

ANGEL BED. A type of bed without posts.

ANTHEMION. Classical Greek honey-

suckle; ornament rather like a palm leaf.

ANTIMACASSAR. A decorative cover placed on the backs of chairs and sofas as a protection against the macassar or other hair oil used by the Victorian dandies.

APPLIED MOULDINGS. Mouldings applied to furniture to suggest panelling; popular during early 17th century.

APRON. A piece of wood, usually shaped, fitted below the frame of a chair or table between the legs or to the base of a cabinet.

ARABESQUE. Painted, carved or inlaid ornament consisting of fanciful interweaving in which scrolls, fruit, foliage and human and animal forms are combined.

ARCHITRAVE. The lowest member of an entablature (q.v.) or main beam resting on the capitals of the columns.

ARK. A wooden chest or box. In early times shaped like Noah's ark. The rougher type was used as a meal bin, but more carefully made arks, fitted with a secret spring, became the 'strong box' for the family treasures and documents. Men who made these chests were known as arkwrights, which survives as a surname.

ARMOIRE. A large cupboard for food and other goods. Also called AMBRY.

ARM STUMP. The vertical front support of the elbow rest of a chair.

ASTRAGAL. A small convex moulding, usually from half to three-quarters of a circle, often carved with bead and reel. Cut with a rectangular step or groove, known as a rabbet (q.v.), and used to hold glass panels for cabinet doors, etc.

BABY CAGE. A contrivance used

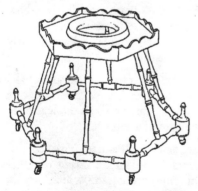

in the nursery to teach a child to walk. Those of the 17th century

were quite simple. In the early 18th century, these 'going carts', as they were called, were considerably improved. One style of which examples still survive, has a top with a gallery. A circular hole is cut in the top and hinged to lift in two semi-circular sections to allow the child to be placed in the circular hole and to be supported when the two sections are lowered. The top is supported on turned balusters which are fixed in a turned spreading hexagonal base with a stout leg on a castor at each of the six angles. This type is moved quite easily in any direction without exertion from the child.

BACK STOOL. An armless chair with upholstered seat and back.

BACON CUPBOARD. Also called a bacon settle. A box-like seat with

a high panelled back; the seat similar to a small chest with either a hinged lid or two deep drawers. The back is a shallow cupboard enclosed by doors and fitted with iron hooks for hanging the flitches of bacon and hams.

BAIL HANDLE. A drawer handle or pull in the form of a loop or ring.

BALUSTER. A light pillar turned in various shapes generally with a square member at each end.

BANISTER BACK. A Hepplewhite chair-back of banisters from seat to top rail. 'Banister' is corruption of baluster.

BANNER SCREEN. An adjustable needlework or other panel on a pole with tripod support, used as a fire screen.

BANQUETTE. A narrow upholstered seat, such as a window seat.

BAR BACK. A Hepplewhite shield-back chair with uprights curved to follow the outline of the shield.

BAROQUE. An extravagant and fantastic style of decoration common during the first part of the 18th century. The outstanding features are heavy curved forms, broken scrolls and decoration borrowed from architecture. Originated in Italy.

BASIN STAND. Small stand of mahogany, either square, round or triangular for a hand basin. 18th century.

BASSET TABLE. Table for the card game of basset which resembled faro. Early 18th century.

BATTEN. A strip of wood fastened across the grain of one or more wide pieces to prevent warping.

BEAD AND REEL. A round moulding with single or double disks alternating with olive-shaped beads.

BEAD-FLUSH. Panel surrounded by a bead let in the edges of a frame so that the faces of panel, bead and frame are flush, i.e. level.

BEADING. A half-round moulding with a series of bead-like projections.

BEARERS. Pieces of wood supporting a shelf in a bookcase or cabinet; also the rails bearing a drawer.

BED STEPS. Set of steps on castors, often with a hand-rail used with the high beds of the 18th century.

BEVEL. A sloping or oblique edge made by cutting away the angle formed by two plain surfaces such as the edge of some mirror plates.

BIBLE BOX. A small box with flat

or sloping lid to hold the family Bible; a similar box with a narrow flat shelf above the sloping lid is a box desk—the ancestor of the bureau.

BIRD CAGE. Name given to a construction used with pillar tables to allow the top to revolve and to be lifted from the pillar. Two bearers are fixed to the underside of the top, spaced to fit snugly on each side of an open boxing; this boxing is formed of two pieces of wood fastened at each corner by a short vertical spindle and is known as a 'bird cage.' The two bearers are

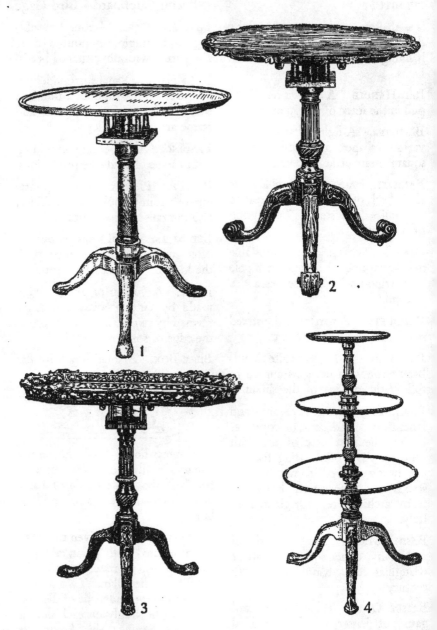

1. Tripod table with plain moulded top and open boxing known as a bird cage
2. Chippendale carved pie-crust table with fluted pillar and scroll feet
3. Chippendale carved octagonal tray-top table with fret ornament
4. Dumb-waiter with three shelves on tripod support

bored to take a pivot on each side of the top plate of the boxing and this allows the top to be tilted. When the table top is down, it is held firm by a spring catch which engages in a socket in the top plate. The top of the pillar is turned and fits in a hole bored in the lower plate of the boxing, the table top being held in place by a wedge driven in a slot cut in the turned section of the pillar. By these several gadgets, the top of the table can be revolved with the bird cage; by releasing the spring catch, it can be tilted; or by removing the wedge, it can be lifted from the pillar.

BIRD's BEAK LOCK. Term applied to locks used with cylinder-front desks, such as the modern roll-top desk, and pianos.

BLOCK FOOT. A square terminal to a straight, untapered leg of a chair or table. *See* MARLBOROUGH LEG.

BLOCK FRONT. A projecting front in curved or square block form

developed during the later 18th century in the United States largely by John Goddard of Newport, Rhode Island and John Townsend of Philadelphia.

BOFFET CHAIR. *See* BUFFET CHAIR.

BOLECTION. A moulding fitting around and projecting beyond the surface of a door or other panel.

BOMBÉ. Convex or bulging shape adapted to English furniture from the French style.

BONHEUR DU JOUR. A French writing-desk of an elaborate character intended for a boudoir; resembles a small bureau and was copied by Hepplewhite.

BONNET TOP. A name denoting a dome-shaped top of a cabinet.

BORDE. The ancient name for a dining-table which consisted of planks supported on trestles. The word survives in board (of directors), bed and board, board wages, boarder, etc.

BOSS. A carved protuberant ornament placed at the intersections of the ribs of ancient vaulting; also wrought in metal and applied as an ornament.

BOTTLE TURNING. A turned shape resembling a bottle introduced from Holland in the William and Mary period.

BOW FRONT. A convex or D-shape popular in the 18th century.

BOW TOP. The top rail of a chair-back which has a low unbroken curve.

c

BOX SETTLE. A settle with a seat in the form of a chest or box with hinged lid.

BRACKET FOOT. A low rectangular

support, often shaped on the inside of the angle, fitted to and projecting slightly from the corner of a chest of drawers, a bureau, a cabinet or other box-like furniture, so that it runs each way from the corner. Used during the 18th century.

BREAK FRONT. Where a large

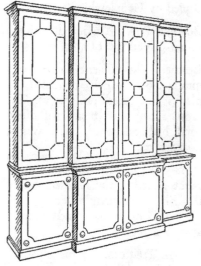

piece of furniture such as a bookcase or similar wall piece has a front broken by one or more sections projecting and others recessed.

BREWSTER CHAIR. A chair with two turned stout pillar front legs rising above a plain wood seat to support arm-rests and two pillar legs at the back continuing upward to form a high back; the back has two vertical rows of turned spindles, a similar row under each arm-rest and two rows of spindles on each side below the seat—known in the United States as a Brewster chair, because one of this type is traditionally thought to have been among the possessions carried over by the *Mayflower*.

BROKEN PEDIMENT. The ornamental

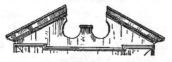

structure, similar to an architectural gable where the sides which would form the top angle of the triangle are not joined; used above the cornice of cabinets, mirrors, grandfather clocks and like furniture.

BUFFET CHAIR. A chair with triangular seat and three turned stout legs, stretcher rails and rails sloping from a heavy top-rail to the front legs extending above the seat; the sloping rails are a primitive form of arm-rest. This type of early chair is a simpler interpretation of the elaborate chairs of Henry VIII's time, referred to in contemporary inventories as 'turneyed' (turned) chairs.

BUN FOOT. A flattened sphere or bun-shape foot of a leg with a slender ankle.

BUREAU. In Great Britain, the word bureau denotes a writing-desk with a fall, a cylinder or a tambour front. In the United States, it is more generally applied to a chest of drawers while the writing-desk is called an escritoire or scrutoire.

BUTLER'S TRAY. A wooden tray, sometimes with hinged sides which can be supported on an accompanying X-shaped folding stand.

CABOCHON. A plain round or oval convex form usually with carved

ornament surround; the cabochon and leaf was popular for some forty years, from about 1725, on the knee of cabriole legs.

CABRIOLE. A leg with a pronounced curve at the knee tapering in a graceful curve to a slender ankle with various shaped feet. Introduced from Holland toward the end of the 17th century and developed to more refined forms during the first half of the 18th century. Said to have been adapted from a goat's leg, the French word *cabriole* meaning a goat's leap.

CAMEL BACK. Term sometimes used to denote a chair with a serpentine top-rail found with shield-back and other chairs of the Hepplewhite school.

CANDLE BOARD. A small pull-out

shelf to hold a candlestick. Used below the cabinet of secretary-cabinets and with card tables.

CANOPY. A projecting fixture over a throne or ancient chair (*see* SEIGNIORIAL CHAIR); also the covering over a four-post bedstead.

CANTERBURY. A low stand with divisions for holding music; also a box-seat with lift top used as a piano seat.

CAPITAL. The head or top member of a column, pillar or pilaster crowning the shaft and supporting the entablature (q.v).

CARCASE. The main body or framework of a piece of case-like furniture, i.e. without doors, veneer or applied ornaments.

CARLTON HOUSE TABLE. A writing table about 5 feet 6 inches long, slightly rounded at the back, a low superstructure with a flat top and fitted shallow drawers and small cupboards.

CARTOUCHE. An ornament imitating a scroll with ends rolled up enclosing a tablet sometimes decorated or inscribed.

Camel Back Chair

35

CARYATID. A female figure used in place of a pillar to support an entablature (q.v.).

CASTOR. Small wheel on a swivel fitted to feet of chairs, sofas, tables, etc.

CAT. A small double-tripod stand, i.e. three pieces of turned wood, crossed and joined at the middle so forming a tripod on which it stands and a tripod above for holding a plate before a fire.

CAVETTO. A concave moulding usually a quarter-circle curve.

CELLARET. A small chest with divisions or a deep drawer, also with divisions, in a sideboard for keeping wine in the dining-room.

CHAIR-BACK SETTEE. A long up-

holstered seat with back formed of two or more open chair-backs and an arm at each end.

CHAISE LONGUE. Literally a long chair. Some are in three parts (two arm-chairs and a stool

between); others similar to a chair with a long seat for reclining.

CHAMFER. A symmetrical cutting away of the right-angled edge where two plain surfaces join to form the angle. The inside angle of square legs of Chippendale furniture is chamfered.

CHANDELIER. A hanging light fixture with several branches for candles; generally of cut glass with pendent cut-glass drops, known as lustres.

CHESTERFIELD. A large overstuffed double-end couch, often with one end hinged to drop.

CHEST-ON-CHEST. *See* DOUBLE CHEST.

CHEVAL GLASS. A mirror about 6 feet high to reflect a full-length figure made to swing from stout pillars with a stretcher and raised on low trestles—the name means literally 'horse glass', being applied because it is large enough to reflect a horse.

CHIFFONIER. A small cabinet with drawer and shelves; also a tall narrow chest of drawers sometimes with a mirror.

CHIP CARVING. A style of carving done by chipping away the wood from the design—often by cutting chips away with a knife.

CHIPPENDALE STYLE. Furniture developed by Thomas Chippendale and other 18th-century cabinet-makers. The name Chippendale, as applied to furniture, implies it is of the school of makers of which Thomas Chippendale was the leader —not necessarily that it was made in

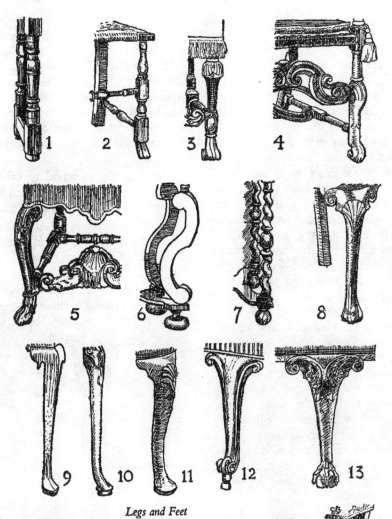

Legs and Feet

1. Plain turned column or baluster;   2. Turned vase member and Portuguese foot, showing leg spiked into seat;   3. Turned taper with inverted cup shape and whorled foot;   4. Shapes derived from Flemish curves;   5. Early cabriole with paw foot, turned rails, and carved front stretcher;   6. Flemish scroll with flat stretcher and bun feet;   7. Spiral turned with flat stretcher;   8 to 13. Types of cabriole showing earpieces, carved escallop shell on knees, the French scroll foot, the claw-and-ball foot, and various forms of plain feet;   14. Square tapered with spade foot and plain back leg with splay his shop on St. Martin's Lane, London. The designs were basically those introduced by the Dutch at the end of the 17th century, refined during Queen Anne's reign and which became more ornamental in the early Georgian period. Earlier Chippendale furniture has features similar to the early Georgian; later, the French, Chinese and Gothic elements were introduced. Legs are square, with the inside angle chamfered, plain moulded or with a fretted design and with stretcher rails between the legs. Cabriole legs carved on the knee frequently with the claw and ball foot though other forms of foot such as the French scroll were used. French influence shows in carved scrolls, and other rococo forms and the scroll or 'fiddle-head' foot; Chinese influence in trellis designs, pagodas and Oriental figures; and the Gothic in various geometrical arches and forms familiar in Gothic architecture. Chair-backs with pierced splats, others carved and pierced in the form of ribbon, called ribbon-back; and with rails suggestive of the rungs of a ladder, known as ladder-back.

Cissing. Wetting woodwork with beer and rubbing it with whiting, so that the colours, which are mixed with beer, will adhere to the surface —a process employed in graining.

Clap Table. Former name for a console or pier table (q.v.).

Claw and Ball Foot. A foot, used with the cabriole leg, carved to suggest a claw of a large bird holding a ball with the underside

flattened slightly. Derived from the Orient and represents a dragon's foot holding the sacred Bhuddist pearl. Introduced to England in the later 17th century in its then quite primitive form. Popular in the United States where the cabinet-makers of Philadelphia developed the claw and ball to a remarkable refinement. *See* p. 37.

Cleat. A strip of wood or other material fastened across a surface to strengthen and hold it in position.

Club Foot. Resembles the head of a club usually with a circular disk about half an inch thick. *See* p. 37, No. 10.

Cluster Leg or Column. Several light columns (usually three or four) passed through moulded blocks of

wood, bored to take them, and— with a leg—ending in a square block foot. Borrowed by Chippendale from the Gothic and used extensively during the Chippendale period, especially by Ince and Mayhew.

Cock Bead. A moulding of rounded beads projecting from an edge; sometimes used on drawer fronts.

Cock-Fighting Chair. A pear-shaped upholstered seat, high padded back with curved arms at the top, in which a lunette is cut. The wealthy cock-fighting enthusiast straddled the seat, resting his chin in the lunette and his elbows on the arms—in other words, he sat facing the back of the chair. Similar chairs for reading (and very comfortable

they are) were fitted with a small book-rest, candle brackets and a pull-out hinged box in each arm to hold tobacco, pipes, etc.

COMB BACK. A name given in the United States to a type of high back Windsor chair with a shaped top-rail similar in outline to the spine of combs at one time worn by women to keep their hair in place. Formed of spindles rising from the seat and passing through the horseshoe-shaped rail of the back.

COMMODE. A chest of drawers often of bombé form and usually of a decorative character—from the French, *commode*, convenient.

COMMONWEALTH. Influenced by the Puritan tenets, furniture of the Cromwellian period became simple and austere. Straight lines and rectangular forms replaced the large bulbous legs of the Elizabethan and early Stuart styles; square underbracing was used, but turned rails were also adopted; chests were fitted with one drawer; gate-leg tables appeared; the feet of chairs and tables were bun or ball shape; and a characteristic decoration was the geometric arrangement of mitred mouldings on the front of court cupboards, chests, etc., the panels sometimes being inlaid with ivory and mother of pearl.

COMPOSITION. A mixture of whiting, resin and glue moulded and used instead of wood carving—also known as stucco.

CONNECTICUT CHEST. An early New England chest with three carved panels and applied split baluster ornaments.

CONSOLE. A bracket, generally scroll shape.

CONSOLE TABLE. A table against a wall supported, partly by two consoles (q.v.) or by ornamental legs resembling consoles—usually with a tall mirror fixed to the wall above; also called pier table.

CONSTITUTIONAL MIRROR. Name applied in the United States to mirrors in walnut or mahogany frames, sometimes with gilt ornaments and surmounted by an eagle. It is commonly suggested that this use of the eagle had its origin in the United States. It was used, however, with mirrors in England as early as Queen Anne's reign. The bird ornament continued popular through the 18th century and later, both in the United States and England.

CONTOUR. The outline of a shape; a moulding, etc., in profile.

CONVEX MIRROR. A wall mirror in circular gilt frame, sometimes with candle sconces and surmounted by an eagle. The convex glass gives an amusingly distorted reflection.

COOPERED. Sections of furniture such as legs consisting of pieces of wood glued together and the joints concealed with veneer.

CORNER BLOCK. Triangular blocks such as are fixed in the angles of chair seat frames to brace them.

CORNICE. The moulding finishing and projecting from the top of a cabinet or similar piece. *See* ENTABLATURE.

CORNUCOPIA. The horn of Amalthea, emblem of plenty; filled with flowers, fruit and corn used as a carved ornament with furniture of the early 19th century.

COURT CUPBOARD. A cupboard,

usually in two tiers resembling a low cupboard placed on a chest or box with panelled doors, as a rule carved; also called standing

cupboard. 17th century. *See* DEUDDARN and TRIDARN.

CREDENCE. Originally a table where food was tasted to guard against poison; later developed to a kind of side table or buffet.

CRENATE. Rounded or scalloped edge.

CRESTING. A carved ornament on

the top-rail of a chair or top of other furniture.

CRICKET TABLE. An early 17th-century table with a triangular frame on three turned legs.

CRINOLINE STRETCHER. A semicircular rail connecting the two front legs and itself connected by two short rails to the back legs; a characteristic of some Windsor chairs.

C-SCROLL. A C-shaped ornament introduced from France and common with English furniture of the first half of the 18th century.

CUCKING STOOL. A crude kind of chair fixed to the end of a long pole which was pivoted. Formerly scolds, dishonest tradesmen, disorderly women and the like were fastened in the chair and ducked.

CUPBOARD. Derived from cup borde, a board or plank on which drinking cups were placed; a cup borde was a series of shelves in

steps, similar to a step-ladder, on which the cups were displayed.

CUP-TURNED. A leg turned in a shape having cup-like member.

CURIO TABLE. A small table with shallow box-like frame top fitted glass panels at sides and hinged, glazed lid.

CURULE. An ancient Roman chair of state with X-shaped supports. The design was adopted during the Empire period. Sheraton bestowed the name 'Curricule' on one of his late chair designs.

CYLINDER. Name applied to a quadrant or arc-shaped fall of a writing-desk—a modern roll-top desk is a development of the earlier cylinder front.

CYMA. A wavy S-like curve. The

brace used in printing is a double cyma. Cyma recta is a concave curve above and a convex below; cyma reversa is a convex above and a concave below.

DARBY AND JOAN SEAT. An 18th-century wide upholstered seat to accommodate two people; also called a love seat.

DAVENPORT. A small writing-desk with hinged sloping writing slab and drawers down the sides of the pedestal; also name given to a divan.

DAY-BED. A development of the late 17th-century straight-back

chair; the chair seat was extended, two extra legs added and the back given a comfortable slope or made adjustable for reclining.

DENTILS. An ornament, frequently in a cornice, consisting of series of equally spaced, square blocks, rather like a row of teeth—hence the name dental from the latin *dens*—tooth.

DERBYSHIRE CHAIR. Chair with arcaded back formed of turned

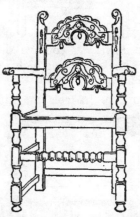

spindles and arches, square uprights, back legs and rails, turned front legs and front rail; also a back with two carved scalloped wide rails, a crescent shape and three pendent drops.

DESK BOX. Box hinged to open and form a sloping surface for writing. Inside fitted with inkpot and compartments for papers, etc.

41

Deuddarn (cwpwrdd). Welsh court cupboard of two tiers. *See* Tridarn.

Diaper. A design of one or more decorative units forming a pattern by being repeated.

Dinner Wagon. Two or three tiers on castors for use in the dining-room.

Dipped Seat. A concave shaped seat, i.e. the sides being higher than the middle.

Dished Top. A table top slightly

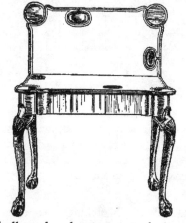

hollowed, so leaving a raised edge; a dished corner is a similar hollow at the corner of a table to hold a

candlestick; small deeper hollows in the top of a card table are 'tills' for coins or counters.

Divan. A large low couch without back or arms.

Dole Cupboard. A medieval food cupboard with pierced ventilation openings in front; also called livery cupboards (q.v.).

Double Chair. *See* Chair-back Settee.

Double Chest. One chest of drawers fitted to and surmounting another chest.

Double-gate Table. A large gate-leg table with two gates to each of the two hinge flaps.

Dovetail. A flaring tenon (q.v.) shaped like a dove's tail which fits tightly into a similarly shaped socket or mortise (q.v.) so forming an interlocking joint. Any well made drawer is dovetailed.

DOWEL. A wooden peg, usually circular for fastening the joint of two pieces of wood.

DOWER CHEST. Name given to large chests made of oak, either plain, carved or inlaid—traditionally the 'bottom drawer' of a medieval bride-to-be.

DRAUGHT-CHAIR. A wooden chair

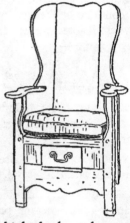

with high back and rectangular wings the entire length of the back the slope of which was adjustable, referred to as a 'sleeping chayre'— later upholstered.

DRAW TABLE. 17th-century table of the so-named refectory type with a pull-out leaf at each end fitted under the top on runners, called lopers, the table could be extended by drawing out these leaves.

DRESSER. A series of narrow shelves on a deep box-like top, fitted drawers supported on legs, usually with a platform close to the floor.

DRESSING CHEST. Chest of drawers fitted with a mirror.

DRESSING TABLE. A narrow table with a fixed or separate mirror.

DRESSOIR. The ancient forerunner of the dresser (q.v.) on which the plate of the wealthy was displayed —described as 'the chief article of furniture in the principal living-room of the great' during the 15th century.

DRINKING TABLE. See WINE TABLE.

DROP-FRONT. The front or lid of

a desk which rests on slides when opened to form a writing slab.

DRUNKARD'S CHAIR. A wide seated arm-chair of proportions suitable for comfortable lolling.

DUMB WAITER. A series of, usually, three circular trays (often revolving) on a pillar and tripod for carrying round the dining table. A similar article with only one shelf on a low pillar for placing on the centre of the dining-table is often called a LAZY SUSAN. *See* p. 32, No. 4.

DUTCH STYLE. The styles which the Dutch developed from the Chinese and were introduced to England by followers of William III in late 17th century and first to

New York and Pennsylvania by the Dutch settlers.

EARLY GEORGIAN. Walnut remained fashionable for furniture until nearly the middle of the 18th century when it was superseded by mahogany after the duty on the latter was discontinued. The simple styles of the previous, Queen Anne, period were replaced by more massive furniture decorated with prominent carved details. The cabriole leg became stouter with a more pronounced curve; the favourite terminal feet were the claw and ball and the lion's paw; the knee of the cabriole was carved with a bold mask, a lion's head or cabochon and leaf; and the ends of the arms of chairs and settees were often carved with a lion's head or eagle's head in full relief. The styles of the contemporary costume are reflected in the furniture; chair seats were made larger and the arm supports slanted sharply backward to accommodate the women's hoop skirts and the men's skirted coats; and the influence of changing social customs is seen in the many small tables demanded by the increasing popularity of tea drinking. The undulating curved or serpentine shape was introduced; and cabinet doors were divided by moulding into small rectangles and glazed.

EARLY STUART. Furniture of the earlier 17th century remained crude in design, the makers being carpenters who worked at building both houses and furniture. Turned legs for stools and the front legs of chairs became general and the gateleg table came into use; arm-chairs had high panelled backs with shaped cresting, carved and sometimes inlaid. The principal furniture, in addition to chairs and tables, were large box-like cupboards and chests, the wood used being almost invariably oak. Few examples of this period have survived.

EARLY TUDOR. *See* GOTHIC AND EARLY TUDOR.

EARS. A small bracket-like scroll shape added to the top of a cabriole leg to continue the curve of the knee, where it joins the seat frame.

EGG AND DART. A moulding of egg-shaped ornaments alternating with darts.

EGG AND TONGUE. An alternate name for egg and dart (q.v.).

ELBOW CHAIR. Any chair with open elbow-rests whether padded or plain wood such as those (sometimes called a carving chair) which are part of a set of dining chairs.

ELIZABETHAN. *See* TUDOR-ELIZABETHAN.

ELLIPTICAL. Having the outline of an ellipse or oval.

EMPIRE. *See* REGENCY.

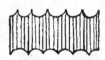

ENGRAILED. Edges indented with small concave curves.

ENTABLATURE. Name given to members above an architectural column, i.e. the architrave, frieze and cornice; as applied to cabinets and similar furniture, generally regarded as the cornice.

ENVELOPE TABLE. A small table having a square top with a right angle, triangular flap hinged to each side; each flap is a quarter of the area of the top, so that, folded, they fit exactly over the latter. When the flaps are open to increase the size of the table, the square top is given a quarter turn bringing each side of the square across an angle of the frame which then supports the flaps.

ESCALLOP SHELL. The radially ribbed shell of the scallop; used as a carved ornament on 18th-century furniture. It is the emblem of St. John of Compostella and of pilgrims to his shrine.

ESCRITOIRE. An enclosed writing-desk, the interior usually fitted with small drawers and compartments—a bureau (q.v.).

ESCUTCHEON. The small brass plate over a keyhole to protect the wood. Also a heraldic shield bearing a coat of arms.

ÉTAGÈRE. The French name for a series of open shelves usually placed in a corner to hold bric-à-brac. *See* WHATNOT.

EVOLUTE. A wave scroll repeated as a frieze.

FALL FRONT. Sloping lid of a bureau (q.v.) hinged at the bottom to fall forward, for use as a writing flap, supported by pull-out slides. Also called DROP FRONT.

FAN-BACK. A chair-back with a straight or undulating top-rail formed of turned spindles—the name sometimes applied to a certain type of Windsor chair in the United States.

FARTHINGALE OR FARDINGALE CHAIR. Chair without arms intended as a seat for a woman during the Elizabethan and James I periods. The name is derived from the voluminous padded skirt called a farthingale.

FEATHER-EDGING. Two bands of veneer or marquetry with the grain of each laid obliquely to suggest a feather pattern.

FESTOON. An ornament, as a garland or wreath of flowers, fruit and leaves, hanging in a series of natural curves.

FIDDLE BACK. Early 18th-century chair with splat shaped somewhat like a fiddle; also the name given to a wavy veneer resembling that used on the back of a violin.

FIDDLE HEAD. Name sometimes used to denote the scroll-shaped foot with the lighter cabriole leg introduced from France. *See* p. 37, No. 12.

FIDDLE SPLAT. *See* FIDDLE BACK.

FIDDLE STRING OR STICK BACK. A back of straight spindles common to Windsor chairs.

FIELD BEDSTEAD. Name given in the United States to a four-post bedstead with a domed or curved tester.

FIGURE. Term denoting the decorative qualities of furniture wood—applied more particularly to the markings of veneers.

FILLET. A thin flat strip particularly a flat moulding separating other mouldings.

FLEMISH CURVE. The sturdy S-shape often used in reverse 2 with the arms, front legs and stretcher of late 17th-century chairs.

FLEMISH SCROLL. A scroll formed of a C-curve joined to a reversed Ɔ and forming an angle—also referred to as the double C-scroll. *See* p. 37, No. 4.

FLY RAIL. The rail at the side of a flap table which pulls out to support a hinged flap; also a bracket for the same purpose.

FOUR POSTER. A large bedstead with four turned wood posts which support the tester.

FRET ORNAMENT. Ornamental pierced work of small designs, such as the galleries of wine tables, panels in clock cases, or forms applied to a solid background. The work is done by a very fine saw. *See* p. 32, No. 3.

FRETWORK. *See* FRET ORNAMENT.

FRIEZE. A flat member of an entablature between the cornice and the architrave (q.v.).

GADROON OR GODROON. A small projecting ornament of a series of convex curves, rather like split almond shapes carved on edges. *See* LOBING AND NULLING.

GARLAND. *See* FESTOON.

GATE-LEG TABLE. Table with fixed top on four legs with stretcher rails and two hinged flaps each supported by a 'gate' which swings on a 'post' pivoted in the frame and a stretcher rail.

GESSO. Composition of plaster of Paris or whiting and size for making bas-reliefs and other ornamentation.

GIRANDOLE. Bracket or candle-holders often fixed to a mirror fashionable during the 18th century.

GOTHIC AND EARLY TUDOR. The principal piece of furniture of this period was the chest or hutch which was used as a seat and as a place to store clothing, family papers and valuables. A few box desks with sloping lids on which a book might be placed have survived from the early period. Tables were merely a narrow board placed on trestles known as a 'borde'. The table at which the master and his principal guests and members of his family were seated was usually a fixture raised on a dais (hence the term 'high table') placed across the end of the great hall; other tables were along the walls in the body of the hall and these when not in use were taken apart leaving the great hall clear for dancing and games. Some of the chests were of the dug-out type, that is, they were hollowed out and fashioned from a large piece of tree trunk. Panels of the chests were carved with tracery and, in addition to the linenfold (q.v.) pattern, the decorative details included a similar carved ornament of a parchment scroll. *See* PARCHMIN.

GOUTY CHAIR. An upholstered arm-chair with a cushioned pull-out foot-rest.

GRANDFATHER CHAIR. Popular name for an upholstered high-back wing chair.

GREEK FRET. A combination of straight lines or bars at right angles repeated continuously to form an ornamental meander (q.v.).

GUERIDON. A small round table or stand on a pillar usually to hold a candelabrum.

GUILLOCHE. Ornamental pattern of

interlaced bands forming circular outlines; suggestive of braided ribbon.

HARLEQUIN TABLE. A multiple table with the top in two folding hinged

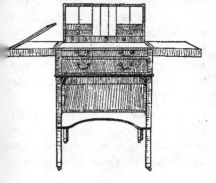

parts, a cupboard under and a small cabinet of pigeon holes and drawers which can be raised or lowered. Invented by Sheraton who says of it: 'This piece serves not only as a breakfast table but also as a writing table. . . .'

HEPPLEWHITE. *See* HEPPLEWHITE-SHERATON.

HEPPLEWHITE-SHERATON. The late 18th-century furniture based upon the designs in George Hepplewhite's *Cabinet Maker and Upholsterer's Guide* and Thomas Sheraton's *The Cabinet-Maker and Upholsterer's Drawing Book*. Both these men and their lesser known contemporaries borrowed from the designs of Robert Adam though modifying the classic ornamentation. Hepplewhite's work is marked by simplicity combined with graceful curves; he was clearly influenced by both the Louis XV and Louis XVI styles. Sheraton was more inclined toward those of Louis XVI as shown by his free use of the turned tapered leg instead of the square tapered. Furniture of the Hepplewhite-Sheraton school depends rather upon surface decoration than upon carving. Finely figured veneers, and lighter coloured woods such as kingwood, satinwood, pear, chestnut and others were used; mahogany was inlaid with small ornaments of lighter wood, the more common being chains of husks, urns and drapery; some furniture was painted and marquetry was also used. Dining tables were of the sectional type on pillars with, usually, D-shaped ends and additional rectangular sections fastened

47

together by brass clips; sideboards were of convenient sizes and of different gracefully curved shapes, chairs for the dining-room were in sets and various delicate occasional tables were made for afternoon tea. Larger furniture such as cabinets, bookcases, bureaux and other pieces, like those for the dining-room, were of a character suitable for the average home as distinct from the stiff formal designs of Robert Adam intended for the palatial apartments of the fashionable world.

HERRING-BONING. A pattern suggesting the backbone of a fish formed by two narrow bands of veneer cut obliquely and placed together.

HIGH-BOY. A chest of drawers

supported on a stand with legs, or on a low-boy (q.v.).

HIGH TABLE. In medieval times the table raised on a dais reserved for the master, his family and principal guests. *See* BORDE.

HITCHCOCK CHAIR. Early 19th-century rush seat chair, with turned legs decorated with stencilled decoration; made by L. Hitchcock. (United States.)

HOCK-LEG. A leg of the cabriole

style with an angle breaking the curve under the knee; it might be described as a reversed letter Ɔ continuing down at an angle vertically.

HOGARTH CHAIR. Name sometimes applied to the early 18th-century walnut chair with the plain splat.

HOOF FOOT. A foot shaped as the hoof of an animal; often called *pied de biche*, hind's foot.

HOOP BACK. The back of a chair where the uprights and curved top rail are a continuous line like the letter ∩ inverted.

HORSE CHAIR. A large arm-chair fitted with strong springs in a very deep seat which was pleated. On days when he could not attend a

Hoop Back Chair

meet or ride, the squire exercised by bumping up and down on his 'horse' chair.

HORSESHOE TABLE. *See* WINE TABLE.

H-STRETCHER. Rails connecting the back and front legs and a rail joining those at the sides forming the letter H.

HUSK ORNAMENT. A small pendent floral ornament used in 18th-century furniture and decoration.

HUTCH. Ancient name for a large chest or coffer—later, a medieval chest with doors on a stand with legs.

INVERTED CUP-SHAPE. Round cup-shaped capping of turned tapering legs. Late 17th century.

JACOBEAN. *See* EARLY STUART.

JOINED OR JOYNED. Woodwork in which the joints were mortised and tenoned (q.v.) and fixed by wood pegs. Joyner was the medieval name for the craftsman who made both furniture and built the woodwork of a house—to-day one is a cabinet maker and the other a carpenter or joiner.

JOINT STOOL. Early rectangular wood stool which was joined (q.v.). 'Joint' is a corruption of 'joyned'.

KAS. A large cupboard occasionally with painted decoration introduced to New York and Pennsylvania by the early Dutch settlers.

KIDNEY TABLE. A table oval in form with a concave front resembling the outline of a kidney—designed by Sheraton.

KNEE. The bulging or convex curve at the upper part of a cabriole leg.

LACE BOX. Small box for lace; usually ornamented with inlay; 17th century.

LADDER BACK. Name denoting a chair which has a series of horizontal slats between the uprights suggesting the rungs of a ladder.

LAMINATE. Wood built in plies or layers; plywood.

LANCASHIRE CHAIR. A chair with

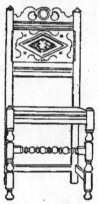

carved panel back open below; square uprights, back legs and side-rails, turned front legs and stretcher.

LATER 18TH CENTURY. *See* ADAM and HEPPLEWHITE-SHERATON.

D

LATE STUART. With the return of the monarchy, the drear days of the Commonwealth gave way to a light-heartedness, which was reflected in the household furniture after 1660. The changes in style were traceable to the many Continental craftsmen who then came to England. The gate-leg table remained popular; chairs had plain and spiral turned legs and uprights and elaborately carved backs, framing a cane panel, and a deep carved rail between the front legs; later padding and upholstery were introduced with seats and backs. Slope front bureaux were made with six spiral legs and flat shaped rails; court cupboards; day-beds and small pieces such as stools came into use. The outstanding ornamental details were various carved scrolls, the whorled or scroll foot (q.v.) and deeply carved back-frame, and front stretcher. Walnut began to replace oak for furniture which did not call for large pieces of wood, but any articles of walnut, dating from the time of Charles II, are relatively few.

LAZY SUSAN. See DUMB WAITER.

LIBRARY STEPS. For reaching high book shelves. Often a low step-ladder concealed in a table or combined with a stool or with a chair.

LINENFOLD. A Gothic carved orna-

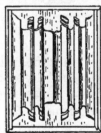

ment representing the folds of linen; it derived from the folded napkin covering the chalice at the consecration of the Host.

LINEN PRESS. A contrivance (similar to a modern letter-press) of two boards with a wood spiral screw about 2 feet long for pressing table linen, etc. In use from about 1650 and in 18th century sometimes fixed to a chest of drawers; the name also applied to a large cupboard fitted with shelves for household linen. See PRESS.

LION MASK. A lion's face carved generally on the knee of a cabriole leg; a lion's head was used occasionally as a terminal to elbow-rests of chairs.

LIVERY CUPBOARD. A cupboard in which food and clothing were kept for retainers. Wynkyn de Worde (1510) describes it as 'open and furnished with shelves whereon the ration called a livery ... was placed.' From the French livrée—delivery; thus, formerly, the clothes delivered to a manservant by his master, i.e., a uniform or livery. See DOLE CUPBOARD.

LOBING. Similar to gadroon (q.v.).

LOO TABLE. An oval gaming table for playing loo, a game played for stakes with three or five cards dealt each player—from the French lanturelu.

LOOSE SEAT. A chair seat upholstered on a separate frame which fits into the seat frame.

LOPER. See DRAW TABLE.

LOW-BOY. A dressing table with several drawers in front.

LOZENGE. A diamond-shaped ornament common with late 16th- and early 17th-century chair backs and other furniture.

LYRE SHAPE. A form used as a

table support, etc.; early 19th century. The shape was from the ancient lyre which was two curved horns.

MARLBOROUGH LEG. Straight square leg with square block foot or plinth.

MEANDER. Any ornamental pattern which may be repeated indefinitely; for example the Greek fret (q.v.).

MEDALLION. A panel or plaque carved with a figure in relief.

MONEY DISH. Shallow depression in the top of a card table to hold coins or counters. See DISHED TOP.

MONK'S BENCH. See TABLE CHAIR.

MORTISE AND TENON. A slot (mortise) cut in one piece of wood into which the end (tenon) of another piece is fitted and the joint secured by wood pegs or glued.

MOTIF. The outstanding or dominant idea in an artistic composition.

MOULDING. A narrow projecting or sunken plain or round surface used for decoration.

MULE CHEST. A large chest with hinged lid and a drawer fitted in the base.

NEST OF TABLES. A set of, usually four, small light tables of varying sizes which slide one into the other when not in use; also called quartette tables.

NONESUCH CHESTS. A chest decorated in various coloured woods with scenes of Nonesuch Palace built by Henry VIII near Cheam, Surrey about 1590.

NOTCHING OR NICKING. A simple form of ornamenting early oak furniture.

NULLING. Similar to gadroon (q.v.).

OCCASIONAL TABLE. Small, light portable tables suitable for the tea-tray and similar uses; various types were introduced in the 18th century.

OGEE. An S-shaped outline; a cyma recta or cyma reversa. See CYMA.

OGEE FOOT. A cyma reversa shaped bracket foot. See CYMA.

ONION FOOT. Name sometimes applied to the oval-shaped bulbous foot of the late 17th century.

ORMOLU. A metal composed of brass and zinc of which mounts for furniture were cast; it is similar to the colour of gold, the name being from the French or moulu, ground gold.

OTTOMAN. Upholstered seat without back or arms; a box with a padded top.

PANEL. A distinct surface of a door or wainscot, etc., raised above or depressed below the level of the frame.

PARCHMIN. Name denoting a Gothic carved pattern taken from parchment scrolls rolled on a rod. It resembles linenfold.

PARCHMENT PANEL. A name sometimes applied to a linenfold (q.v.) panel.

PATERA. A small round or elliptical ornament resembling a shallow dish carved in low relief and applied to furniture.

PEDIMENT. Strictly, the triangular part usually over the portico of ancient architecture. Name now applied to any part, triangular or scrolled, etc., suggestive of an architectural pediment as the cresting of a cabinet, bookcase, mirror, or similar piece.

PEMBROKE TABLE. A table with a

relatively wide fixed top and flaps on each side supported on hinged brackets; generally on four legs but later on pillar support.

PIE-CRUST TABLE. Name given to small table with slightly dished top and the edge raised and scalloped;

usually a round top, on pillar and tripod. *See* p. 32, No. 2.

PIER TABLE. *See* CONSOLE TABLE.

PIER GLASS. A large wall mirror placed above a pier or console table (q.v.).

PIGEON HOLE. Small open compartment or recess in a desk or cabinet for keeping papers.

PILASTER. A rectangular, upright, flat pillar, which projects slightly; applied to the front of taller furniture.

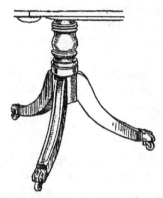

PILLAR AND CLAW. Term denoting the pillar and claw feet of tables of the late Georgian period.

POLE LATHE. *See* WINDSOR CHAIR.

POLE SCREEN. A small frame usually with needlework panel on a tall pole and tripod.

POWDERING STAND. A tripod stand with three supports rising from the legs with a moulded rim to hold a small basin; immediately above the base is a dished platform for a water jug and, between that and the basin, two small triangular drawers. These stands were intended to be placed in a corner and to-day are placed in a corner with the basin filled with flowers. Also called BASIN STAND.

PRESS. A cupboard generally used for household linen. See LINEN PRESS.

PRIE-DIEU CHAIR. Chair for praying with high back and padded top for resting the elbows; low upholstered seat to kneel upon.

PRINCE OF WALES FEATHERS. Three ostrich plumes copied from the badge of the Prince of Wales used as a decoration by Hepplewhite.

QUADRANT. Quarter circle metal support used with the fall fronts of some desks.

QUARTETTE TABLES. See NEST OF TABLES.

QUATREFOIL. A design with four lobes; for example a four-leaf clover.

QUEEN ANNE. The early years of the 18th century marked the establishment of middle-class houses and the introduction of convenient and comfortable furniture. The designs were relatively simple and the construction sound. Walnut was used almost exclusively either in the solid or, for larger surfaces, in veneer on an oak carcase. Marquetry which had been popular in the later 17th century declined and was restricted to small panels. Carved ornament was employed, but this too was restricted to small motifs in low relief. Splats and chair frames were veneered with figured wood and decorative effects were achieved by this means with bureaux, drawer fronts and other large surfaces. The various styles

of legs characteristic of the preceding period (see WILLIAM and MARY) disappeared excepting the cabriole which was now considerably refined. During the early years of Queen Anne's reign, turned understretchers continued to be used with chairs, but these were eventually discarded. Upholstery became a permanent feature with all seats and also with backs of some dining chairs. Card-playing and gaming became fashionable and card tables were in demand. Structural features of the period were the slight curving of seat fronts of chairs, settees, etc.; chair seats narrowed from front to back; and the backs had broad fiddle-shaped splats and were spooned to fit the body.

QUINCUNX. A pattern formed of five objects placed one in the centre and one at each angle of a square.

QUIRK. A channel or groove separating a bead moulding from adjoining members.

RABBET OR REBATE. A rectangular channel or groove cut in the face or edge of a piece of wood to receive another piece, such as a panel or a sheet of glass.

RAIL. The horizontal member of a door or panel frame. See STILE.

RAKE. The inclination or angle from the perpendicular; the slope.

RANCE. The cross rail between legs of a chair.

READING CHAIR. See COCKFIGHTING CHAIR.

REEDING. A series of small convex moulded members—the reverse of flutings.

REFECTORY TABLE. A long narrow table on heavy legs with stout stretcher rails close to the floor. The name originated from the long table used in the refectory or dining-hall of early monasteries.

REGENCY. English early 19th-century furniture was strongly influenced by the French Empire style before the Prince of Wales became Regent in 1811, but the new designs became fashionable during the Regency for which reason the latter designation seems more appropriate. The furniture of this time shows a gradual grafting of the French Empire forms upon those of the English late 18th century; this is shown in *Sheraton's Cabinet Dictionary*, published in 1803 and in other contemporary books of designs. One of the characteristics of the period (in addition to the free use of Egyptian symbolic forms), was the extensive employment of brass —apparent in the frequency of small brass columns; cast brass lion-paw feet; large lion-head handles; pierced brass galleries on low cabinets and writing tables; fine brass lines inlaid; and often an elaborate pattern cut from thin brass inlaid in a veneered surface. The favourite wood was rosewood. Among more prominent designers of the period were: Henry Holland, Thomas Hope, Thomas Sheraton and George Smith.

RENAISSANCE. The revival or re-birth of the classic styles in Italy during the 14th century which spread through other European countries reaching England in the 16th century and eventually superseding the Gothic forms.

RENT TABLE. The name given to

the round or octagonal revolving drum-top table on pillar support, fitted drawers, labelled dates or days and sometimes a cupboard in the pillar for account books.

RIBBON-BACK. A chair-back pierced and carved to resemble interlaced and tied ribbon; a feature of more elaborate Chippendale chairs.

ROCAILLE. *See* ROCOCO.

ROCOCO. A style developed in France by Juste-Aurèle Meissonier from the Chinese forms. Shell-work and scrolls dominate the ornament combined with marine subjects, ribbon, flowers, heads, busts and rustic subjects. It was interpreted in England by the designers and craftsmen of the Chippendale school.

RONDEL. Any circular form used as a ground for ornament. *See* MEDALLION, PATERA, ROSACE.

ROSACE. A circular ornament usually enclosing a rosette.

ROUNDABOUT CHAIR. This term is applied to any chair where the arms and back form a semi-circle —the familiar office desk-chair on turned legs and stretchers is an example. As a rule the seat is lozenge-shape or circular; one leg is in front, one at each side and one at the back, the three last mentioned extending upwards to support the semi-circular back rail.

RUDD'S TABLE. One of the ingenious pieces of multiple furniture of the later 18th century; designed by Hepplewhite, who called it 'Rudd's Table' or 'Reflecting Dressing Table'. It has a centre drawer fitted with a sliding top for writing and compartments under; on each side is a narrow drawer also with compartments and each fitted with a mirror which folds over and slides under the top of the table when the drawers are closed. Thomas Shearer shows a similar table in his *Household Furniture 1788*.

RULE JOINT. A joint similar to that in a carpenter's folding rule; it is used with table flaps and may be recognized by the rounded member which fills the gap when the flap is down.

SADDLE SEAT. A shaped dipped chair seat left thicker at the centre front, suggesting the pommel of a saddle—used with Windsor chairs.

SCROLL. An ornament more or less imitating the spiral of loosely coiled parchment or a curled foliated form.

SCROLL FOOT. A volute scroll foot introduced from France. *See* FIDDLE HEAD.

SCRUTOIRE. *See* ESCRITOIRE.

SECRETAIRE. A writing-desk similar to an escritoire (q.v.) with a bookcase or cabinet above.

SEDAN CHAIR. An enclosed vehicle to accommodate one person, carried on poles by two chairmen. 17th and 18th centuries.

SEIGNIORIAL CHAIR. Ancient throne-like seat with arms, high back and canopy. In medieval times, there was rarely more than one chair in a house and that was strictly reserved for the master as the one in authority. Its significance survives in 'The Chair' and 'Chairman'.

SERPENTINE SHAPE. An undulating curve adapted to the front of furniture.

SERRATED. An edging notched like the teeth of an ordinary saw.

SETTEE. A long low seat with back and arms upholstered.

SETTLE. A long wooden seat with an arm at each end and a high panelled back; the lower box-like part was sometimes fitted with drawers or a hinged lid. *See* BACON CUPBOARD.

SHERATON. *See* HEPPLEWHITE-SHERATON.

SHIELD-BACK CHAIR. A shield-shaped back, usually with rounded

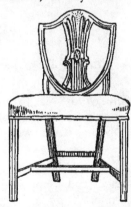

base, the serpentine or 'hump' top rail and pierced splat; a more

elaborate back is heart shape some-
times called the interlaced shield.
These chairs are associated with the
Hepplewhite school.

SHOE OR SHOE PIECE. Shaped
member projecting from back rail
of a chair-seat frame to which the
base of the splat is fitted.

SIDEBOARD. Formerly a side-borde
or serving table. In the later
18th century, Robert Adam placed
a pedestal fitted with a cupboard
and surmounted by a large urn at
each end of the table; one of the
cupboards held wine bottles and the
other was lined with metal and
fitted with iron racks and a small
tripod to hold a thick piece of hot
iron to keep the plates and food hot.
Later the three pieces were joined
and the various types of sideboards
were developed.

SIDE CHAIR. Term used to denote
a small chair without arms or
elbow-rests.

SLAT. The horizontal bars or rails
between the uprights of a chair-
back.

SLAT-BACK CHAIR. See LADDER
BACK.

SLEEPING CHAIR. See DRAUGHT
CHAIR.

SOFA. The word 'sofa' (from the
Arabic *soffah*, a bench) denotes a
long upholstered couch with back
and raised end.

SOFA TABLE. A table with a hinged
flap at each end, supported on
trestles connected by a stretcher;
introduced by Sheraton; later examples on pillar support.

56

Sofa Table

SPADE FOOT. A tapered foot with
four equal sides each resembling
the shape of a spade; used with the
late 18th-century square tapered leg.

SPARVER. Ancient term for a curtain
fixed to a bed or used in a room;
also a canopy of a bed.

SPINDLE. A slender turned baluster
or rod used in making furniture or
applied as an ornament. See SPLIT
BALUSTER.

SPINNING CHAIR. Name given to
a wooden seat with a detachable
narrow back supposedly made for
use with a spinning wheel.

SPLAT OR SPLAD. The vertical
member (usually shaped) in the
centre of a chair-back connecting
the back rail of the seat with the top
rail.

SPLIT BALUSTER. A baluster or

spindle split lengthwise and each
half used as an applied ornament to

the front of a chest or similar piece. 17th century.

SPOOL TURNING. A turned bulbous or other pattern repeated continuously.

SPOON BACK. Chair-back having a spoon-like concave curve fitting the contour of the body—early 18th century.

SPRING EDGE. The upholstered edge of a seat made more comfortable by resting on springs instead of on a wooden frame.

SQUAB SEAT. A loose cushion for a chair; a deep stuffed cushion suitable for a low seat or foot-rest.

STANDARD. Term used to denote the uprights supporting a swing mirror.

STILE. The vertical member in a door or a panel frame. *See* RAIL.

STRAP WORK. Carved ornamental design of narrow bands crossed and interlaced; popular during the Elizabethan, and early Stuart periods.

STRETCHER. A rail connecting and bracing the legs of a chair or table, etc.

STUCCO. *See* COMPOSITION.

STUDS. Nails with large metal heads placed closely to form a design.

STUMP BEDSTEAD. A name sometimes applied to a bedstead without posts or tester.

SUTHERLAND TABLE. A low table with narrow fixed top and two wide hinged flaps which are supported on pull-out legs similar to the 'gate-table' principle.

SWAG. An ornament in the form of pendent drapery or festoon of flowers and leaves—the word 'swag' formerly meant to sway or swing.

TABLE CHAIR. A shallow box seat on turned legs continuing up to support stout arms; a back of short boards is fixed to heavy cleats and pinned to each arm, so that, when raised, the boards serve as a high back and when lowered to rest on the arms, the chair becomes a table; 17th century, also called a Monk's Bench.

TABOURET. A small seat, a stool; name also denotes a small stand.

TALL-BOY. One chest of drawers placed on another. *See* DOUBLE CHEST.

TAMBOUR. Thin strips of wood

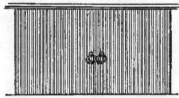

glued to strong canvas to form a flexible door or cover to close vertically or horizontally—the lid of the modern roll-rop desk is a form of tambour.

TEAPOY. A, usually ornamental, box with lift lid containing tea caddies, on a pillar and tripod.

TENON. *See* MORTISE.

TERN FEET. The word 'tern' (meaning set of three) is used to describe the feet formed of three scrolls.

TESTER. A canopy over a bedstead with high posts—a half tester is a canopy covering only half a bedstead.

THERM LEG. A name sometimes applied to the tapered square leg with four-sided or spade foot (q.v.). *See* p. 37, No. 14.

TIER. One of several similar things placed one above the other, as with a series of shelves.

TILL. A shallow saucer cut in the top of card tables. *See* DISHED TOP.

TOP RAIL. The rail between the uprights at the top of a chair back.

TRACERY. Ornamental design found in Gothic windows; appears in furniture of the Chippendale period and in the late 18th-century cabinet doors.

TRAY-TOP TABLE. A small table with a pierced gallery round the top. *See* p. 32, No. 3.

TREFOIL. An ornamental feature of the Gothic style; similar in outline to a three-leaf clover.

TRESTLE. *See* TRESTLE TABLE.

TRESTLE TABLE. Originally a board

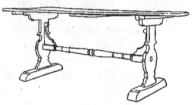

on heavy supports known as trestles which was the dining table or 'borde' of medieval times. The trestles were replaced by legs in the 16th century. *See* BORDE and HIGH TABLE.

TRIDARN (CWPWRDD TRIDARN). Welsh court cupboard of three tiers the upper one an open shelf with canopy above. *See* DEUDDARN.

TRIPOD. A three-leg support used

with a pillar for tables, fire screens, etc.

TRUCKLE-BED. A very low bed frame on small wheels that could be pushed under a large bed. Formerly a servant-attendant slept in one of these beds placed at the foot of the master's bed—Shakespeare refers to 'His standing bed and trucklebed'. Also called trundle-bed.

TUDOR-ELIZABETHAN. During this period improvement in furniture was due to the Italian craftsmen brought by Henry VIII to England; these men introduced the Renaissance arts which gradually replaced the crude Gothic forms. English furniture of this period was carved so excessively there was a lack of plain surface to show off the decoration; the furniture was strongly constructed, the characteristic features being large bulbous members with the legs of tables, and other supports and heavy rectangular understretchers. Chairs were few and those that were made were mostly in the form of a small panelled-chest with a panelled back and arms (*see* WAINSCOT CHAIR). Chairs were few because they were still reserved for the use of the master and mistress, others being seated on a form, a stool or one of the large chests. Among the principal carved ornaments are the Tudor rose, lozenge shape, fruit, flowers and the linenfold (q.v.) on panels. Head-boards of beds were of panels and the massive bed posts were elaborately carved.

URN. A classic vase shaped receptacle placed on the pedestals of a sideboard; also used as a finial ornament with a pediment. The urns employed by Adam were to hold rose-water or fitted small partitions for forks, spoons and knives.

VASE SPLAT. A chair splat resembling the outline of a vase.

WAINSCOT CHAIR. An early massive box-like chair with arms and high back made of wood similar to wall panelling called wainscot.

WARDROBE. The 18th-century wardrobe was in two sections, the lower one a chest of drawers and the upper a press or cupboard fitted with sliding trays enclosed by two doors. In the 19th century a full length hanging cupboard was added to each side of the earlier wardrobe and was known as a wing wardrobe.

WASHSTAND. Our ancestors seem to have substituted powder and rouge for soap and water, so saving themselves the bother of washing; for washstands did not appear until about 1750. Chippendale designed some elaborate examples but the earliest approach to a washstand was the attractive little powdering stand (q.v.). Later in the 18th century other small washstands, usually for standing in a corner, were produced together with pieces combining a washstand and a dressing table known as 'harlequin' furniture.

WELSH DRESSER. A dresser, fitted drawers on turned baluster legs united by pierced and carved aprons.

WHATNOT. A light piece of furni-

ture with a series of shelves to hold bric-à-brac. See ÉTAGÈRE.

WHEEL-BACK CHAIR. Name used to denote a chair of the Hepplewhite

school with an oval (sometimes circular) back with spokes radiating from a small central ornament.

WHEEL CHAIR. Chair with circular seat and semi-circular back on six legs with radiating stretchers resembling the spokes of a wheel.

WHORLED FOOT. Sometimes called paper-scroll, the direction of the scroll turns under, i.e. from front to back, to form a terminal foot on the front legs of late 17th-century chairs. See p. 37, No. 3.

WILLIAM AND MARY. The elaborate furniture of the late Stuart gave way to simpler styles. Traces of the Stuart remained for a while in the carved ornamentation of the high-back chairs. Gradually the former rectangularity was superseded by the curved forms which were the forerunners of the splendid designs of the first half of the 18th century. Several features are peculiar to the William and Mary period, among them, the inverted cup shape often with the plain or octagonal trumpet-shaped leg and the flat serpentine stretcher. Spiral and plain turned supports continued to be used and the Flemish scroll. The cabriole leg came into favour about 1690 when the flat serpentine stretcher gradually passed. One of the immature forms of the cabriole adopted at this time was the so-called hock leg (q.v.). The high-back wing chair in its more comfortable padded form was known, but was not in general use until the early 18th century. The Dutch craftsmen who came to England after the arrival of William III introduced various convenient pieces of household furniture and improved many in general use.

WINDOW-SEAT. An upholstered seat with no back made to the length of and fitted into a window recess.

WINDSOR CHAIRS. A descendant

of the buffet or boffet chair (q.v.) composed of turned members with a saddle-seat (q.v.). Until fairly recently the industry of making these chairs was centred in the woods around High Wycombe. The chairmakers called 'bodgers' buy the beech trees, split them and turn the chair parts with a primitive pole lathe which they set up in a

'wigwam of thatch'. A pole with plenty of spring is selected and fixed to the roof; the pole furnishes the upward pull on a cord passed round the piece of wood to be turned, the counter-pull being made by the 'bodger's' foot on a treadle.

WINE TABLE. Late 18th-century round tip-top table on pillar and tripod; fitted to the top was a raised platform in which holes were cut to fit decanters and goblets; wine glasses were hung by the foot in notches cut in the edge of the table. Another larger wine table of the early 19th century was horseshoe shape for placing by the fireside or in a window recess. This had coasters for the decanters and bottles attached to a metal rod or sliding in a well—doubtless to avoid accidents as the evening advanced and hands became unsteady; most of the horseshoe tables had a net-bag supposedly for biscuits, though it suggests a convenient receptacle for empty bottles; they also had a firescreen to protect overheated guests from the fire.

Oak Chair. Yorkshire or Derbyshire

WINGED BOOKCASE. The term 'winged' is applied to a large bookcase with a break front (q.v.).

YORKSHIRE CHAIR. 17th-century chairs of the type known as Derby-shire chairs (q.v.) are also known as Yorkshire chairs.

YORKSHIRE DRESSER. A dresser with a low back, i.e. without the shelves. See DRESSER.

BIBLIOGRAPHY

BINSTEAD, HERBERT E.: *English Chairs*. 1923.

CESCINSKY, HERBERT: *English Furniture of the Eighteenth Century*. 1911. 3 vols.

—— *The Old-World House*. 1924. 2 vols.

—— *The Gentle Art of Faking Furniture*. 1931.

JOURDAIN, MARGARET: *English Decoration and Furniture of the Later XVIIIth Century (1760-1820)*. 1924.

—— *Regency Furniture (1795-1820)*. 1948.

LENYGON, FRANCIS: *Furniture in England from 1660 to 1760*. 1924.

MACQUOID, PERCY: *History of English Furniture*. 1904. 4 vols.

MACQUOID, PERCY and EDWARDS, RALPH: *The Dictionary of English Furniture from the Middle Ages to the Late Georgian Period*. 1924-27. 3 vols.

PERCIVAL, MACIVER: *Old English Furniture and its Surroundings, from the Restoration to the Regency*. 1920.

SYMONDS, R. W.: *English Furniture from Charles II to George II*. 1929.

TIPPING, H. AVRAY: *English Furniture of the Cabriole Period*. 1922.

—— *Old English Furniture*. 1928.

WENHAM, EDWARD: *The Collector's Guide to Furniture Design*. 1928.

—— *Old Furniture in Modern Rooms*. 3rd Edition. 1951.

BOOKS RELATING TO AMERICAN FURNITURE

CORNELIUS, C. O.: *Early American Furniture*. 1926.

—— *Furniture Masterpieces of Duncan Phyfe*. 1922.

DREPPERD, CARL W.: *Handbook of Antique Chairs*. 1948.

DYER, W. A.: *Early American Craftsmen*. 1915.

HALSEY, R. T. H. and TOWER, ELIZABETH: *Homes of our Ancestors*. 1925.

HOLLOWAY, EDWARD STRATTON: *American Furniture and Decoration*. 1928.

HORNOR, WILLIAM MACPHERSON: *Philadelphia Furniture*. 1935.

LOCKWOOD, LUKE VINCENT: *Colonial Furniture in America*. 1926.

LYON, IRVING WHITALL: *Colonial Furniture of New England*. 1892.

MILLER, EDGAR GEORGE: *American Antique Furniture*. 1937.

NUTTING, WALLACE: *Furniture Treasury*. 1928-33. 3 vols.

ORMSBEE, THOMAS HAMILTON: *The Story of American Furniture*. 1934.

FURNITURE WOODS, VENEERS, MARQUETRY AND INLAY *

ACACIA. Yellowish-brown to reddish tones, hard and durable.

AMBOYNA. Light yellowish-brown to orange in colour; hard with mottled and curled figure. Used in 18th-century furniture for inlaid panels or bandings and occasionally larger surfaces.

ANNUAL OR GROWTH RING. A tree increases its girth yearly by growing a new layer of wood on the outside immediately under the bark. (*See* SAPWOOD.) The growth ceases as the season becomes unfavourable, namely, as winter approaches, so that each year's addition is shown more or less distinctly by a mark called the growth ring. The age of a tree which has been felled may be ascertained by counting the irregular concentric markings showing in the stump (the short piece left standing) or in the butt.

APPLE. Yellowish-brown colour, hard and heavy. Was used in small pieces of country-made furniture and by early American Colonial cabinet-makers.

ASH. Light yellow, tough, strong and very tensile which allows it to be bent. Used in 18th-century furniture, particularly for the hooped backs of Windsor chairs.

BANDING. Framing a veneered panel with strips of veneer of a contrasting, usually straight, grain and colour shade.

BEECH. Yellowish-white to light reddish-brown. One of the harder woods; when quarter or nearly quarter cut, the medullary rays (q.v.) show as dark flakes. Chiefly used for seat frames, bent chairbacks, seat rails and runners for rocking chairs. Beech is particularly liable to the ravages of wood-boring worms.

BIRCH. Yellowish often with attractive figure. When quarter cut, medullary rays show as reddish-brown flakes. Used extensively for cheaper furniture when it is stained to resemble mahogany. The pores (i.e. the tiny fine grooves) as seen in a plain sawed longitudinal surface, such as the top of a desk or table, are barely visible to the naked eye, whereas those of mahogany are seen clearly.

BIRD'S EYE. This mysterious figure results from indentations in the annual rings (q.v.). When cut through tangentially, the series of circlets, somewhat like a bird's eye, are produced. These circlets or tiny swirls grow radially and when distributed in the light wood, result in an attractive and valuable veneer. Occurs mainly in maple, but sometimes in walnut and a few other woods.

BLISTER. A rare figure due to an uneven contour in the annual rings or other freak growth; it occurs in mahogany, poplar and pine. Used as a veneer.

BOULLE. The name given to a style of veneering developed by the French cabinet-maker, Charles André Boulle (1642-1732). It consists of inlaid designs of metal and tortoiseshell and sometimes ivory and enamelled metal. The process proved very costly owing to the large amount of expensive material wasted in cutting and the time lost in sawing each little pattern separately. Later, Boulle evolved a more economic method. Equal numbers of thin sheets of metal and of tortoiseshell were pinned together and, by sawing through the bundle, it was possible to produce an equal number of ornamental shapes, such as flowers, scrolls, etc., of each material. In this way, each metal shape could be dropped into the corresponding space in the tortoiseshell and vice versa. This latter method is known as counter-boulle—to an extent, it might be likened to that of making jig-saw puzzles. The word boulle is not infrequently spelled 'buhl'.

BOXWOOD. Yellowish shade, very tough close texture. Used for inlay.

BROKEN STRIPE. Where the stripe or ribbon figure runs for about a foot and then disappears, it is known as broken stripe; if it is in shorter lengths, it is roe.

BURR OR BURL. Overgrown knot or other abnormal growth on a trunk of a tree. Walnut burl is cut from old trees and has a figure resembling innumerable curly and wavy twirls interspersed with darker brown. Burls also occur with cherry, maple, oak and some other trees.

CAMPHOR WOOD. Has the aromatic smell of camphor and is used for lining chests.

CEDAR. Soft brown fragrant wood. Used for the lining of chests, cupboards and for drawers as its pleasant aroma protects fabrics from being attacked by moths and other insects.

CERTOSINA. A style of mosaic in geometric shapes of bone or ivory inlaid in a dark wood.

CHERRY. Pinkish colour, very close grain, hard and strong. When old, the colour resembles mahogany but lacks the figure. The pores are much smaller than those of mahogany and hardly visible, the medullary rays being seen only on a quarter cut surface. Used in Britain for chairs and panels during the 17th and 18th centuries, though few examples remain; used to a greater extent by American Colonial cabinet-makers for simpler pieces and some furniture was made of cherry wood in the United States in the early 19th century.

CHESTNUT. Structure similar to oak, but has not the large rays. White and fairly hard, but not sufficiently hard for rough wear. Used for cores which are veneered, drawer linings and inlay.

CROSS-BANDING. *See* BANDING.

CROTCH. Veneer cut from the part of a tree where a large limb joins the trunk or where twin trunks join—thus at a fork or crotch. It produces a peculiar plume-like figure, when matched, such as is seen with doors of sideboards, grandfather clocks and other large surfaces. *See* MATCHING.

DEAL. Term now generally used in Britain to denote fir or pine wood. Its strict meaning is a board of fir or pine cut to one of any specified sizes; standard deals from which others are sawn are usually 9 inches wide, 3 inches thick and 12 feet long; whole deals are $1\frac{1}{2}$ inches thick; slit deals $\frac{5}{8}$ inch thick; five-cut stuff $\frac{1}{2}$ inch or less. Pieces less than 6 feet are known as deal ends.

EBONY. Hard heavy wood varying from jet black; it may be streaked with reddish-brown, creamy-white, pink or variegated shades. Grandfather and other clock cases of oak were veneered with ebony in the 17th century; mostly used for inlay, piano keys and small work. Some of the finest ebony comes from southern India and Ceylon.

ELM. Tough wood strongly marked; employed for furniture in medieval times but is now restricted to seats of chairs of the Windsor type.

FIDDLE-BACK. Wavy veneer resembling the figure of sycamore commonly used in the back of a violin.

FIGURE. The term used for the design in woods resulting from cutting across distorted fibres, such as an overgrown knot, a root, a crotch or other irregular growth.

FIR. The silver fir growing freely in the mountains of central and southern Europe. Soft white wood valued for carving and for making stringed instruments.

FLITCH. Strictly this term means the outside slice cut from a tree trunk; in cabinet-making, it is the name for a section of a log cut in thin sheets showing the figure. The sheets are laid together in a bundle in the order they are sawn or sliced and the bundle is known as a flitch. *See* VENEER.

GRAIN. The fibre forming the actual substance of a tree; the natural lines of wood showing no abnormal figure.

HAREWOOD. *See* SYCAMORE.

HOLLY. White or greyish-white, hardwood used mostly for inlay as it takes a smooth surface when polished.

HORNBEAM. Close-grained white wood, very tough and hard, difficult to polish so is seldom used for furniture.

INLAY. The term inlaid is used

generally where inlaid, lighter wood is subsidiary and the greater part of the surface is the darker ground; as for example, a mahogany sideboard with the drawer fronts, and perhaps the top, outlined by a strip of some lighter wood such as holly, technically known as stringing.

KINGWOOD. A Brazilian wood also known as violet wood from the violet tone of its markings. Used with fine cabinet-work as a banding during the late 18th century.

KNUR. A hard excrescence on the trunk of a tree:

LABURNUM. The heartwood (the centre of the trunk) of laburnum is dark brown with a subtle greenish tone; the sapwood (the outer, youngest part of the trunk immediately under the bark) is yellowish. The annual rings are very distinct for which reason laburnum was used for the 'oyster' veneer during the late 17th century and after. See OYSTERING.

LIME. A soft white tree with virtually no cross grain. During the William and Mary and Queen Anne periods it was employed for the elaborate carved work of Grinling Gibbons and his followers.

MAHOGANY. A map of the sources of mahogany shows widely separated habitats, each of which produces a different variety. In the Americas it thrives in Southern Mexico through Central America to Venezuela and Northern Columbia; it also grows in Cuba and Santo Domingo and in more recent years it has been found in north-west

Brazil and Peru. African mahogany comes from the Ivory Coast, Gold Coast and Nigeria; and some is produced in Ceylon. It is said that this wood was first brought to England by Raleigh in 1595. When it was introduced for furniture (about 1725-30) it was the Santo Domingo or Spanish mahogany as it is called. This West Indian mahogany is close grained with a silky texture; when newly sawn it is yellowish-white, but exposed to sunlight and air it changes to golden brown or brownish-red. To-day it is very scarce. The mahoganies from Mexico, Central and South America have a close family resemblance one to the other; when newly sawn the wood ranges from yellowish-white to salmon pink, changing when exposed to light and air to a golden brown. African mahogany is obtainable in very large logs; it also offers a greater variety of figures than other mahoganies, for which reason it is largely converted to veneer. The name mahogany is conferred on several woods which are used as cheaper substitutes. To distinguish the real from the imitation is not always easy. Birch is one of the imitations, but with this the pores are very fine, whereas those of mahogany are a distinct series of dots or dashes according to whether it was cut across or with the grain. Where the substitute is a tropical wood— such as one of the Asiatic Dipterocarpus family—it may be recognized by the pores being larger and the grain very noticeably longer and coarser. Again, while the pores of

B

all genuine mahogany contain a dark deposit in scattered quantities, this is not present in the Asiatic woods. With a lens the deposit can be seen readily on unfinished woods, and usually even when wood has been filled and polished. Where wood described as mahogany shows a fiddle-back, mottle, broken stripe or crotch, it may be accepted as the 'real thing'. There are some woods which resemble the characteristics of mahogany sufficiently closely to be mistaken for it, for instance Spanish cedar (cigar-box wood), padouk, (an Asiatic red wood).

MAPLE. A close grain white wood, the pores of which are invisible unless magnified. It is used for inlay with marquetry. The annual rings of maple are made definite by a brownish layer. See BIRD'S EYE.

MARQUETRY. A decorative design of contrasting woods or other material, dyed to obtain the various colour tones, inlaid in a background of dark veneer and glued to the carcase which was usually oak.

MATCHING. Term denoting the fitting together of two adjacent, but reversed sections of figured veneer to form a symmetrical 'design' or 'complete face' as it is called. For example—diamond-pattern and the plume-like effects, such as are to be seen on the doors of sideboards and like fairly large panels; there are various other patterns achieved by matching veneers.

MEDULLARY RAY. This ray radiates outward from the heart of a log forming a 'sunburst'. In cutting

66

logs into flitches (q.v.) the side of the flitch should run parallel to the ray. The rays of oak are larger than any native wood and are seen as the silver grain or splash of quartered oak.

OAK. This tree comes under two main classes, i.e. evergreen and deciduous, each of which includes a number of species. The evergreen or ilex, known as the holm oak, thrives in the South of England, and in Mediterranean countries; the wood of the holm is very heavy and hard and shows some figure if sawn radially. The so-called English oak is one of the longest-lived trees and highly valued for its timber. Another is the Durmast oak which is found wild in Britain, and there are numbers of hybrids. The Lucombe oak which, it is said, was first planted at Exeter in the mid-18th century, has glossy green leaves covered on the underside by a greyish felt. Oak was used for furniture almost exclusively until the second half of the 17th century when walnut became fashionable; but even then oak continued to be used for carcases which were veneered with walnut, and for furniture made in provincial shops. Oak is one wood which probably the majority of people readily identify and there is a fairly general familiarity with the curious splash which is the result of quartering. See MEDULLARY RAY.

OLIVE. A close-grained wood, yellow, or of a curious greenish-brown tint with dark veinings. It takes an excellent polish and was used in the early marquetry decoration.

OYSTERING. A decorative surface achieved with slices cut transversely from small boughs or saplings which show irregular concentric rings— annual growth rings (q.v.)—cut from laburnum or walnut.

PADOUK. A wood with a silky texture tinged with red similar to rosewood, a very heavy tough wood; a native of the Andaman Islands first imported to England in the early 18th century.

PARQUETRY. Geometrical pieces of wood, sometimes coloured, fitted together and glued to a bed or core; used for tops of backgammon tables, etc., and floors.

PEAR. Hard close-grained showing no figure; colour ranges from yellow to brown, sometimes with a reddish tinge. Stained black and carefully finished, has the appearance of ebony.

PINE. The so-called Scotch pine which is widely distributed in Europe was the wood called yellow and red deal, used for panelling rooms during the 18th century; its particular feature is its knotty character which adds to its ornamental qualities. The carcases of veneered case furniture were often made of pine and it is used for drawer linings and in place of more expensive wood.

PITCH PINE. A pine tree (pinus rigida) common in Canada and the United States. A very heavy strong wood, yellowish with reddish-brown streaks in the grain. Rarely used in furniture.

POLLARDING. Cutting away all branches of the top or crown of a tree. This causes a larger number of branches to grow and when a tree has been pollarded annually for some years, irregular growths occur and unusually figured veneers are produced from those sections of the tree. Pollarded surfaces were used during the early 18th century.

PORES. The minute tubes through which a tree draws nourishment from the roots; they are visible to a greater or lesser extent in a finished board, according to the particular wood.

PURPLE HEART. A native wood of northern South America; hard, elastic and heavy; when newly cut it shows a distinct purplish tint, but this becomes brown when exposed to the atmosphere. Very rarely used in furniture except as inlay and sometimes for quite small ornamental articles.

QUARTER-CUT. A tree trunk has both annual rings and rays (q.v.). Consequently it can be sawn or cut, as we say, in two different ways (a) along, that is parallel to, the rays from the outside through the centre of the trunk producing what is called quarter-sawn timber, (b) or plain-sawn at right angles with the rays and roughly parallel with the rings. Quarter-sawn timber or veneer has a noticeably more ornamental figure than plain-sawn especially oak, mahogany and some other hardwoods—most softwoods produce a better figure when plain-sawn.

ROSEWOOD. Grown largely in

Brazil and in the East Indies, this wood is named from its fragrant odour which is pronounced when it is newly cut. It is extremely hard and heavy with a relatively straight grain. The prevailing colour is brown or purplish-brown with dark, almost black streaks. Used for furniture, especially during the early 19th century.

SABICU. Produced from a large tree grown in Cuba; mahogany red colour, very heavy, hard and durable—it was selected for the stairs of the 1851 exhibition in London, and despite the millions of feet that trod those stairs in six months, the wood showed virtually no signs of wear. Some furniture was made of sabicu, but specimens are rare.

SANDALWOOD. A highly fragrant wood found chiefly in Southern India; very hard, yellowish-brown and close-grained. Used largely for carving, and for making small boxes and fans; the veneers employed widely for inlays. The oil obtained from distilling the wood is used as a perfume.

SAPWOOD (Alburnum). The outermost and newest grown wood of a tree, immediately beneath the bark, by which the sap rises. The heartwood in the centre of a tree trunk is much harder and is called the duramen.

SATINWOOD. There is East Indian or Ceylon and West Indian satinwood. The former is light yellow to golden brown and highly figured with a satin-like lustre; it grows to a large size but frequently develops

defects. It is used mainly as a veneer. The East Indian satinwood seems not to have been used to any extent until the 19th century; that used by the late 18th-century cabinet-makers being the West Indian variety. Both are similar in character though the West Indian is not as figured, and it is a more uniform yellow; also it has a pleasant odour.

SEAWEED MARQUETRY. An early 18th-century intricate design of the arabesque style.

SNAKEWOOD. A very hard wood of a yellowish-brown with irregular darker patches suggestive of a snake skin or crude writing. As a rule used for inlaying and banding, but some furniture was made of snakewood at the end of the 18th and early 19th century. There is a set of chairs at Mason & Co., the well-known pottery.

STRINGING. Narrow lines of light coloured wood inlaid.

SYCAMORE. A yellowish-white wood of the maple family. Often shows a fine figure; used for backs of violins (see FIDDLE BACK) and the interior of furniture. Sycamore, soaked in water and stained with oxide of iron takes on a greenish-grey tone, and is called 'harewood'.

TEAK. A wood without any distinctive figure that grows in India, Hindustan, Malay, Burma, Java, etc. A golden-brown colour, fairly hard and heavy. Very little used for furniture in the Western world.

THUYA. One of the handsome evergreen shrubs in English gardens, but in the eastern United States it reaches 50–60 feet. The wood which is used in veneers, is a golden brown after being polished, 'spotted' with 'bird's eyes' in disk-like outlines.

TULIPWOOD. A native of Brazil; tulipwood is yellowish with purple or pinkish-red stripes, very hard and heavy. It is used for inlaying, though the available supply of the wood is small.

VENEER. Thin sheets of wood sawn or sliced from various parts of a tree which will give a figure. See BURR, CROTCH, FLITCH, OYSTERING.

WALNUT. This wood was introduced to England in the 16th century, but was not used for furniture until about a hundred years later, i.e. the last half of the 17th century when chairs were made of it. The early years of the 18th century came to be known as the Walnut Age, as it was the fashionable wood for furniture until the coming of mahogany (q.v.). Walnut is fairly hard and takes a fine polish; like purple heart, when newly cut it has a distinct purple tone, but after exposure to light, it becomes a soft brown.

The attractive burr (q.v.) figure is produced by walnut and cut into veneers, and oyster pieces are cut from the saplings of walnut grown in the Eastern United States, commonly called black walnut which is darker and harder than the English.

YEW. This familiar evergreen produces a hard, close-grained elastic wood of a reddish-brown colour, and yellow sapwood. It is insect proof, very durable and may be highly polished; was at one time fairly widely used for hooped-back Windsor chairs; and yew trees were pollarded and used in burr veneers. The yew tree was planted in churchyards, because being evergreen, it was regarded as a symbol of immortality, a belief held by the Druids who planted it near their temples.

ZEBRA-WOOD. This rare wood is native of British Guiana where it is known as 'Hyawaballi'. It is striped with contrasting light and dark browns in what might appear to be parallel lines; the wood is used for cross-bandings. It is also called marble wood.

BIBLIOGRAPHY

BROWN, NELSON C.: Forest Products, Their Manufacture and Use. 1919.

DULY, SIDNEY J.: Timber and Timber Products. 1924.

ELWES, HENRY JOHN and HENRY, AUGUSTINE: Trees of Great Britain and Ireland.

HARTIG, R.: Timbers and How to Know them.

KNIGHT, E. V. and WULPI, MEINARD: Veneers and Plywood. 1928.

KOEHLER, ARTHUR: Properties and Uses of Wood. 1924.

SNOW, CHARLES H.: The Principal Species of Wood. Their characteristic properties. 1908.

STONE, HERBERT: Timbers of Commerce and Their Identification.

WELLS, PERCY A.: Veneering, Marquetry and Inlay. 1904.

GLASS ✮

AIR TWIST. A form of decoration used mostly with stems of 18th-century glasses. It was developed from a row of bubbles called 'tears'; the bubbles were pricked and the hole then closed, after which, the stem was drawn out and, at the same time, twisted thus forming the spiral threads of air. The opaque white or the coloured twists were produced by arranging, at intervals, short lengths of slender white or coloured canes (rods) round the inside of an iron cylinder, the inner wall of which was ribbed; then clear metal (molten glass) was forced into the cylinder when the canes united with the molten glass. This combined mass was then twisted and drawn out to a cane (rod) of the desired diameter.

ALE YARD. A glass drinking cup, usually in the form of a coach

horn, about a yard long and known as a 'glass yard of ale' or an 'ale yard'.

AVENTURINE. A type of glass containing tiny gold-coloured spangles originally produced accidentally when some brass filings fell into a pot of molten glass; the name is derived from the French *par aventure.*

BACCARET GLASS. Glass works founded at Baccaret, France. Famous for crystal glass and for the faceted, millefiore and other styles of paperweights, some of which are inscribed B with the date—others bear the date only.

BATTLEDORE. A long, flat, square-end wooden blade for flattening bottoms of glass objects.

BEILBY GLASS. Glass painted by William and Mary Beilby, brother and sister, of Newcastle, England, in the second half of the 18th century. Their decorations range from armorial subjects, both actual and imaginative, landscapes, etc., in colour to scenic subjects, birds, butterflies and the like in white;

others picture the English country-side and various outdoor sports such as fishing, shooting, and hunting. There is a slight bluish tint with the white enamel which is characteristic of the Beilby's painting.

BLOWING-IRON OR BLOW-PIPE. A long iron tube on the end of which a glass-blower gathers a quantity of metal (molten glass) from the crucible which is blown to a bulb and later shaped. *See* BLOWING AND SHAPING GLASS.

BLOWN-MOULD GLASS. *See* MOULDED GLASS.

BLOWING AND SHAPING GLASS. Before the metal (molten glass) is ready for the glass-blower, the temperature of the furnace is lowered to bring the glass to a semi-liquid consistency—rather like heavy treacle. This allows it to be coiled on the end of the heated blowing iron when the blower gathers the mass of glass (called a parison) to the amount required from the crucible; the parison then is rolled on a metal or stone slab, known as a marver. The blower's working tools are quite simple. In addition to a blowing-iron, he has a solid iron rod (punty or pontil) to which the blown glass is transferred from the blowing iron for shaping and finishing; U-shaped spring tools with wooden ends or cutting edges similar to sugar tongs; a compass for measuring and marking; a long square-end wood blade (battledore); a pair of scissors; measuring sticks and various moulds. As a rule, the work is

done by small groups of two or more men (the head man being called the gaffer) and a boy. Each group is known as a 'chair', a name given to the bench with flat, slightly sloping arms on which the glass worker sits, and which serves as his lathe. After the parison is blown and transferred to the punty (iron rod), the punty is balanced on the arms of the 'chair' and rolled to and fro with the hand and shaped by the blades of the 'sugar tongs' in the other. The blown bulb can be shaped to an extent while still on the blowing-iron; if the iron is held upright with the bulb at the top, the bulb 'falls in' and becomes depressed or flattened; held downward, it becomes longer and thinner; and other shapes are achieved by swinging the iron in different ways by experienced blowers. *See* also CROWN GLASS AND MOULDED GLASS.

BOHEMIAN GLASS. The Bohemian glassworks are actually more famous for their fine crystal than for the plentiful, more familiar, red glass decorated with vine leaves and grapes, etc. Some of the deep-cut heavy articles were cast in moulds. The ruby-red glass was perfected in the late 17th century by a chemist named Kunckel who discovered ruby glass had to be heated twice and that only a very small amount of gold had to be used to obtain the colour. Black silhouettes on gold or silver ground and painted designs were all used as decoration. Until the later 19th century, Bohemian glass was produced in small furnaces located in forests where wood was easily obtainable. Afterwards, however, the industry was organised and expanded and the output of cut crystal and coloured glass as well as of novelties such as pipes, walking sticks, etc., gradually increased to enormous quantities, the larger part of which was exported. During the five years 1876 to 1880 the exports to the United States alone amounted to some 3 million dollars (£600,000).

BRISTOL GLASS. During the second

half of the 18th century, upward of twenty glass factories were operating in Bristol, England, producing table glass both clear and coloured blue, purple, green and red. The coloured wares were often decorated with designs in gold, but with many examples this has tended to wear off over the years. The now keenly sought opaque white made at Bristol is unusually attractive, particularly that decorated by the painter Michael Edkins who sometimes used Chinese subjects. Witch balls, rolling pins, pipes, walking sticks and other novelties were made

in fairly large numbers at Bristol; also paperweights, some of which are of greenish glass, during the 19th century. The influence of the Bristol glass-makers is clearly seen in the products of other English and Irish factories; and it spread to America where it shows itself very plainly in the clear and coloured glass made at the works established by Henry William Stiegel at Manheim, Pennsylvania, where both the glass and the style of decorations closely resemble those of Bristol. *See* NAILSEA.

BULL'S EYE. Window glass was formerly known as crown glass which was made by blowing a parison to a large bulb. This bulb when transferred to the punty (iron rod) was spun rapidly in front of a hot furnace causing the bubble to burst and, after a time, expand to a large flat disk or 'crown' as it was called. After being annealed, the crown was cut into glass for windows, but the part that had been fastened to the punty was marred by a protuberance with a 'knot' or 'bull's eye' in the centre left after the punty was broken away from the glass.

BUMPING GLASS. Another name for firing glass (q.v.)

BURETTE. A graduated glass tube usually fitted with a stopcock for measuring small quantities of liquid or gas.

CAMEO GLASS. This form of ornamentation was produced by Thomas Webb of Stourbridge in about 1876. The process more generally used was to coat a layer of white opaque

Glasses decorated with subjects in enamels by Wm. & Mary Beilby

Jacobite engraved glasses. Air-twist stems

Glass engraved portrait William III. Air-twist stem

with a thick layer of blue transparent glass and to cover the blue with a coating of white. The figures and other forms were lined out on the white and the remainder cut away to leave the blue showing as a background; the figures, etc., being carved to sharpen and bring out the details. Another slightly earlier method developed by Apsley Pellatt of Southwark, London, was a form of incrustation. The ornamental subjects used by him were of a classic character—figures, medals, coins and the like—which were moulded in low relief of a composition of kaolin (china clay) and super-silicate of potash—a mixture which will withstand a higher temperature than glass before fusing. The moulded cameo was put into an open glass 'pocket' which was then closed to protect it; or, if quite small, the ornament was applied hot to a heated glass article and covered with metal (molten glass). Some of Pellatt's cameos were enamelled and others treated to resemble silver or gold.

CANE. Name denoting a slender rod of glass such as was used with the coloured twists. See AIR TWIST.

CARAFE. Glass bottle for holding water at table.

COIN GLASSES. Denotes a wine glass with a coin enclosed in the knop of the stem or in the foot. In the United States, the term is also applied to modern pressed glass decorated with replicas of United States coins. The making of these reproduction 'coins' was later forbidden by the authorities.

COCKLE. Wrinkles from contracting in glass.

CORK. See IRISH GLASS.

CRIMPING. Fluting or giving glass a wavy form.

CROWN GLASS. Blown window glass as distinct from glass plates. See BULL'S EYE.

CULLET. Broken or refuse glass remelted as part of the mixture for new glass, the quality of which is improved by the cullet. The piece of glass which remains on the end of the pontil was formerly called a collet.

CUT GLASS. Glass is ornamented by cutting and polishing to bring out its brilliancy. The cutting is done by pressing the glass against the edge of a revolving wheel or disk. Deep cuts are made by an iron wheel fed with sand and water or by a carborundum wheel. Lighter cuts are made by fine sandstone wheels fed with water, which are also used for smoothing the rough surface left by the iron wheels. The glass is polished on wooden wheels fed with wet pumice-powder and rotten-stone (q.v.) and brushes and putty-powder (q.v.). All the wheels are power-driven.

DIAMOND. The decoration which George Ravenscroft, the 17th-century glass-maker called 'nip diamond waise' was known many centuries before his time by nipping together parallel trails; a similar ornament was moulded.

ENGRAVED GLASS. Inscriptions, views and other decoration on glass was done by diamond-engraving and wheel-engraving. W. A. Thorpe says, the diamond was used occasionally for finishing the lettering of a wheel job, but it did not belong to the wheel-cutter's craft. The wheels for making designs on glass are of copper ¼ inch to 2 inches in diameter and are fed with fine emery and oil. Glass is also decorated by two other methods, i.e. sandblast and etching. In the former, the design is subjected to sharp sand driven against the surface by compressed air, the parts to be left plain being covered to protect them against the sand. In the etching process, the glass is dipped in a resinous paint or wax and when this covering is dry, the design is scratched through with a pointed tool and the glass then exposed to hydrofluoric acid which attacks the exposed design.

ETCHED GLASS. *See* ENGRAVED GLASS.

FINGER BOWL. A glass bowl to hold water for rinsing the fingers at table during dessert. A relic of the times before forks were used at table and food was lifted to the mouth with the fingers and each guest dipped his fingers in a silver bowl of rosewater carried by a servant and another servant dried them on a towel.

FIRING GLASS. A small glass with heavy walls and a very thick glass base. They were used at convivial dinners largely for pounding on the table when applauding a speaker. The term 'firing glass' has some connection with what is called Kentish Fire which was expressing approval by stamping the feet on the floor 'three times three and one more'. The expression is said to have come from the wild, prolonged cheering of the anti-papist speakers in Kent in 1828-29.

FLASHING. Covering white glass with a superficial coating of coloured glass; when coloured throughout, it is known as pot-metal.

FLINT GLASS. Good everyday table glass often referred to as crystal glass. Flint glass as understood to-day is a composition of silicates of potash and lead, producing the brilliant colourless glass. The fact that powdered flint was used in making this glass long ago would explain the term 'flint' and to-day all fine glass is equally entitled to be called by that name.

FRIT. The material of which glass is made after being partly fused in a furnace.

GAFFER. The foreman of a chair, namely a bench with flat slightly sloping arms manned by three men and one boy.

GLASS POT. Name given to the crucible in which the materials for making glass are fused.

GLASS SOAP. Actually manganese dioxide or other substance which is added to molten glass to remove the traces of green colour produced by iron salts in the sand.

IRISH GLASS. Glass-works were established in Ireland at Waterford, Cork, Dublin, Belfast and smaller centres during the second half of the 18th century. All the more important works were started by

Englishmen who employed skilled English workmen, which makes it the more surprising that there are those who can distinguish Irish from English glass! That well-known authority Dudley Westropp mentions that Cork and Waterford factories were worked by Stourbridge glass-makers and all the materials came from England. The glass made at these Irish factories, at least during the early period, was, therefore, Stourbridge glass produced in Ireland. The same authority also points out that Waterford glass does not have the blue tint ascribed to it. 'This,' he says, 'in itself stamps as spurious hundreds of pieces which have been accepted as genuine Waterford.' This famous old glass does, however, show varying tints, which, it has been said, were what the glass-makers sought to remedy and collectors insist upon admiring; after the American Revolution, very large quantities of Irish glass were exported to the young Republic and an appreciable amount has been preserved by different American families. A number of glass-houses were working in Dublin, one of the more important being the Round Glass House. This glass-house was the offspring of a glass-works established in Dublin by Phillip Roche, Richard and Christopher Fitzsimons in about 1690. The Round Glass House ceased in 1787. Like those of most Irish factories, the Dublin products have a soft surface and are brilliant. The Cork Glass House and the later Waterloo Glass House each produced excellent

glass, a third works starting in 1818, but neither of the three could withstand the taxes and, after some sixty years, glass-making in Cork finally ceased in 1841. Glass-houses were also started at Ballycastle, Newry and Londonderry, but little is known of their history or their products.

JACOBITE GLASSES. These glasses are connected with the lingering sympathy for the Stuarts during the 18th century. What may be termed the standard Jacobite glass is engraved with a rose and one or two buds; several other emblems were used, including an oak leaf and a thistle. Some glasses are engraved with the portrait of the Old Pretender (James Francis Edward) or the Young Pretender (Charles Edward); verses of a Jacobite song; AMEN; FIAT; REDEAT or similar pious sentiments. The AMEN glasses when original are splendid examples of engraving, for they bear a royal crown, the cipher I.R. (James Rex) incorporating the figure 8 and, generally, some verses of the Jacobite anthem, ending with *Amen*. But as was remarked by one enthusiast, there are good forgeries and a motley collection of reproductions of all these romantic glasses, so 'tis very well to apply the adage *caveat emptor* and seek the advice of experience.

JAMESTOWN, VIRGINIA. First glass-house in America started about 1610. Beads were produced and used in strings for trading with the Indians. The records of the Virginia Company suggest that skilled workmen were sent to Jamestown to work in the glass-house.

KICK. The deep convex at the bottom of a moulded bottle to lessen its capacity; familiar in wine bottles.

LATTICINIO. Fine canes or threads of varicoloured glass forming a filigree effect often used as the background of millefiore (q.v.) in glass paper-weights.

LIPPER. A wooden tool used by a glass-maker in forming a lip or rim of a vessel.

LUSTRE. Name given to pendent glass prisms of large candelabra and smaller candle holders.

LOOKING GLASS. See MIRROR.

MARVER. A polished slab of iron or stone on which the parison (q.v.) is rolled to shape it.

MILLEFIORE. The name (thousand-flowers) given to a form of decoration made by arranging short lengths of various coloured rods of glass—known as canes—fusing them together then cutting them transversely and either embedding the section in clear glass or joining them—used largely with glass paper-weights.

MILK-WHITE GLASS. See OPAQUE WHITE.

MIRROR. Looking glass was first made in England by Sir Robert Mansell at Lambeth about 1624 under a patent granted in 1623. The early mirrors have bevelled edges following the Venetian custom, the glass plates being backed by a film of tin amalgam. A thin sheet of tin-foil thoroughly cleaned and smoothed, was rubbed lightly with mercury, and sufficient mercury was poured on the foil to float the glass; most of the amalgam was then squeezed out by weights on the glass and later the glass was turned, amalgam side up, and allowed to harden. To-day mirror surfaces are made mostly with a coating of pure silver. Mirrors are either plane, convex or concave. The first gives a normal reflection; a convex shows objects distorted and smaller than natural; and in a concave, at a certain distance, objects appear magnified and upside-down.

MOULDED GLASS. Where the shape of a glass object is not spherical it can be made only by blowing a hollow bulb into a mould and so by pressure forcing the glass to take the desired shape; ornamental patterns may be impressed on the surface by the same process. See PRESSED GLASS.

MULE. A name used to denote the foot of a wine-glass.

NAILSEA. The glass-houses at Nailsea are especially associated with the painted lines and loops in different colours. J. R. Lucas of Bristol started making glass at Nailsea Heath in 1788. Glass-makers were brought from France and Lucas produced jugs, carafes, large bowls, single and double flasks, rolling pins, toys, pipes and other articles. The articles were variously decorated with splashes and spots in white and colours laid on in swirls, spirals or loops. Some of the flasks are painted with the ribbon or latticinio effects, the colours employed being greens, blues, red, pink, brown, yellow and white.

NIPT DIAMOND WAISE. *See* DIAMOND.

OPAQUE-WHITE. This is believed to have been made at Bristol before 1750. It was obtained by adding a very small amount of tin oxide to the ordinary flint composition. This opaque-white which was introduced to compete with porcelain is remarkably thin and delicate. It was used largely for covered vases copied from Chinese porcelain originals and decorated in colours in the oriental style as interpreted by the Bristol painters. Articles for general household use, made of opaque-white glass, covered a wide range, and included particularly fine candlesticks, sugar-bowls, cream-jugs, scent-bottles, knife handles, cruets which were often fitted in a wood frame and many others painted by the various artists of whom Michael Edkins was the foremost. This glass was also made at Stourbridge and later at other factories.

PARISON. The mass of molten metal taken from the furnace on the end of the iron. *See* BULL'S EYE.

PONTIL. *See* PUNTY.

POT-METAL. *See* FLASHING.

PRESSED GLASS. This differs technically from moulded glass (q.v.). Pressed glass is shaped in a mould under pressure of a plunger operated by a hand lever, while with moulded glass the pressure is that of a man blowing or of compressed air. The mechanical press-moulding is more successful with such articles as dishes, bowls and similar open and flat shapes.

PUCELLAS OR PROCELLAS. A spring tool similar to, but larger than, a pair of sugar tongs for shaping a glass object as it is rotated on the punty (q.v.).

PUNTY or PONTIL. Iron rod to which the blown glass is transferred from the blowing iron. The punty is balanced on the arms of the chair (*see* GAFFER) and rolling it backward and forward the glass-worker shapes the glass bulb at the end of the iron. The curious circular broken off piece under the base of a glass, called the pontil mark, was left when the punty was separated.

PUTTY POWDER. An oxide of tin used in polishing glass, etc.

ROTTEN-STONE. Decomposed siliceous limestone used for polishing glass and metal.

RUMMER. Large glass on short straight stem; the bowls vary in shape; came into use about 1770.

SHIP DECANTER. Decanter with very wide bottom rather squat conical shape body and fairly long neck. They are little affected by a rolling ship; in really rough weather, it is customary to dampen the tablecloth with water to give the decanter a better 'grip'.

TEAR BOTTLE. Name sometimes given to tiny glass phials which are confused with the so-called tear bottles found in ancient Roman tombs.

TRIPOLI. *See* ROTTEN-STONE.

WATERFORD. *See* IRISH GLASS.

WITCH BALL. A blown varicoloured ball sometimes silvered which was hung at the entrance door or window of cottages as a charm against 'ghosties, ghoulies and beasties'.

BIBLIOGRAPHY

BLES, J.: *Rare English Glasses of the 17th and 18th centuries.* 1926.
BUCKLEY, F.: *History of Old English Glass.* 1925.
DILLON, E.: *Glass.* 1907.
DREPPERD, CARL W.: *ABC's of Old Glass.* 1949.
HARTSHORNE, A.: *Old English Glasses.* 1897.
PELLATT, A.: *Curiosities of Glassmaking.* 1849.
POWELL, H. J.: *Glassmaking in England.* 1923.
THORPE, W. A.: *English and Irish Glass.* 1927.
—— *A History of English and Irish Glass.* 2 vols. 1929.
—— *English Glass.* 1935.
WESTROPP, M. S. D.: *Old Irish Glass.* 1920.

PEWTER, COPPER, BRASS *

ALLOY. Two or more metals united, usually by fusion.

ANDIRONS. *See* FIREDOGS.

ANTIMONY. Metal used in alloys.

AQUAMANILE. A brass ewer in various forms.

BELL METAL. A hard alloy, three or four parts of copper to one of tin used for bells, mortars and standard weights and measures.

BRASS. An alloy of copper and zinc.

BRITANNIA METAL. Introduced about 1769 when it was an alloy of tin, with 5 per cent. of antimony and 1 per cent. of copper.

BRONZE. An alloy of pure copper and tin. To clean bronze, wash with soap and water using a soft cloth or brush, but do not scrub the metal.

CANDLEBOX. A sheet metal, usually brass, box for hanging on the wall to hold spare candles.

CHESTNUT ROASTER. A brass box-shaped container with perforated lid and handle.

CHIMNEY CRANE. An iron bracket hung on the wall of the chimney to swing over the hearth; pot hooks were attached for suspending cooking utensils.

CHOPIN. A Scottish measure holding $\frac{1}{2}$ pint.

CLOCK JACK. A contrivance which when wound turned the spit on which a joint of meat was roasted before an open fire. *See* HASTENER.

COPPER (cleaning). Use paste of powdered-chalk mixed with methylated spirit; rub this on the copper and allow spirit to evaporate leaving the chalk dry; then rub off the chalk and polish.

DAMASCENE. Inlaying steel or other metal with silver or gold.

ESCUTCHEON. Metal plate to protect the wood round a keyhole.

FIREBACK. A heavy iron plate, cast, usually with ornamental front, placed against the wall at the back of the large open hearth fires to radiate the heat.

FIREDOGS. Supports for a log of wood in an open hearth. Originally, stood in front of the huge backlog and carried a smaller log called the firestick.

FOOT-WARMER. Sheet iron or tin-plate box, with holes punched in the sides and top, set in a wood frame with wire handle for carrying. It was filled with hot coals when travelling.

GARNISH. Pewterer's term for complete set of a dozen platters, a dozen dishes and a dozen plates.

GEMELLIONE. A metal basin formerly used for washing hands at table.

GODDART. Name for a tankard or a drinking cup. Corruption of the French, *godet*, a cup.

GRIDIRON. An iron utensil similar to a small grating for broiling food over an open fire.

HAND-WARMER. Brass or copper small spherical box finely pierced containing a piece of hot iron which could be lifted out for heating.

HASTENER. A half-round metal reflector for concentrating the heat on a joint of meat roasting on a spit in front of a fire. *See* CLOCK JACK.

HOLLOW WARE. Term denoting pewter tankards, measures, pots and other vessels to hold liquids.

HORSE BRASSES. Fretted and engraved ornaments of brass; regarded as a charm. With earlier examples, the designs are quite ancient symbols, and these were cut from solid metal and engraved, the forms being replicas of symbols understood by the Saxons, Early English and other older races. Later brasses were stamped or cast.

LATTEN. A medieval brass alloy of copper and zinc formerly used for ecclesiastical utensils.

LOGGERHEAD. Name given to a circular pewter inkstand with hinged cover to the inkpot.

LORIMER. A maker of bits, spurs, and bridle mounts.

MARKS. *See* 'SILVER' MARKS and TOUCH.

MEASURES. Pewter measures were in a set of eleven of various capacities up to a gallon.

MORTARS. Early mortars were usually cast by bell founders of metal used for bells and these will give forth bell-like sounds when struck; later examples were cast in brass and turned on a lathe. With their accompanying pestle, mortars were used for pounding drugs and spices.

MUTCHKIN. A measure of 5 gills (Scottish).

PAKTONG. A Chinese alloy of copper, nickel and zinc; it closely resembles nickel-silver.

PATINA. A fine film or colour resulting from age.

PEWTER. An alloy of tin and other metals, the quality of pewter is determined by the proportion of tin. Thus, old fine pewter is 112 parts of tin to 26 parts of copper; average good pewter is 100 parts of tin to 17 of antimony or to 4 of copper and 8 of antimony; and the low grade metal of the quality used for ale pots in tap rooms known as black metal, only 60 parts of tin to 40 of lead. The copper and the antimony were added to harden the metal.

PEWTERERS' GUILD. The Worshipful Company of Pewterers was founded in 1348 to control and regulate the craft and to ensure that the standard of the metal was maintained. Guilds were also established at Dublin, Cork, Edinburgh, Glasgow and at various English provincial centres.

PINCHBECK. An alloy of five parts of copper to one of zinc, used as an imitation of gold; invented by Christopher Pinchbeck (d. 1732).

PIRLIE-PIG. A Scottish money box, often made of pewter.

RAPE. A coarse rasp, such as a nutmeg-grater or tobacco rasp.

ROASTING JACK. See CLOCK JACK.

SADWARE. Pewter chargers, dishes, plates and similar heavy ware.

'SILVER' MARKS. Marks imitating the hall-marks used on silver were used by pewterers during the 17th century.

SOLDER. Alloy which melts at low heat for making joints of metal.

SPINNING. Shaping a piece of metal by rotating it on a lathe and forcing it with a long steel tool against a 'chuck', namely a shape previously turned in wood of the article to be made.

TAPPIT-HENS. Vessels holding two Scottish pints (equal to three English quarts) or more. Strictly, the name applies to the size holding one Scottish pint, and is derived from the supposed resemblance of a knob on the lid to a crested hen (Scottish tappit-hen).

TINDER BOX. A metal box in which some very inflammable material, such as scorched linen, was kept. The tinder was in the bottom of the box and a hook-shaped piece of good steel was struck by a piece of flint making a spark which fell on the tinder; by blowing, the tinder ignited and a light was obtained by touching the point of a match to the tinder—the matches were thin slivers of wood dipped in melted brimstone. The boxes were of various sizes; those for household use ranging to about 15 inches in length and those for carrying in the pocket 2 to 3 inches.

TOUCH. The mark of the maker stamped on pewter ware; a date appearing with a touch mark denotes the year in which the mark was registered. A considerable quantity of English pewter was not marked.

TRIFLE. Name applied to low grade pewter. See PEWTER.

TRIVET. A small three-legged metal stand for a kettle or other vessel, placed by the fire.

TUTANIA. A tin-base alloy with about 15 per cent. of antimony and a small amount of copper, lead and zinc. Invented by William Tutin of Birmingham, about 1780.

TUTENAG. A Chinese white alloy of zinc, copper, nickel and a small amount of silver or arsenic It resembles German silver.

WORSHIPFUL COMPANY OF PEWTERERS. See PEWTERERS' GUILD.

WRIGGLED WORK. Name given to decoration of pewter done with a flat tool or a scorper held at an angle and pushed along the surface of the metal with a regular rocking action.

BIBLIOGRAPHY

BELL, MALCOLM: *Old Pewter.* 1920.

BURGESS, F. M.: *Chats on Old Copper and Brass.* 1914.

COTTERELL, H. H.: *Old Pewter. Its Makers and Marks.* 1929.

—— *Pewter Down the Ages.* 1932.

COTTERELL, H. H. and WESTROPP, M.: *Irish Pewterers.* 1917.

GALE, E. J.: *Pewter and the Amateur Collector.* 1910.

GARDNER, J. STARKIE: *English Ironwork of the XVII and XVIII Centuries.* 1911.

GOODWIN-SMITH, R.: *English Domestic Metalwork.* 1937.

HENDLEY, T. H.: *Damascening on Steel and Iron.* 1892.

LINDSAY, J. S.: *Iron and Brass Implements of the English House.* 1927.

MARKHAM, C. A.: *Pewter Marks and Old Pewter Ware.* 1928.

MASSE, H. J. L. J.: *Chats on Old Pewter.* 1921.

MICHAELIS, R. F.: *Antique Pewter of the British Isles.* 1955.

MURPHY, B. S.: *English and Scottish Wrought Ironwork.* 1904.

TAVENOR-PERRY, J.: *Copper and Brass.* 1910.

WENHAM, EDWARD: *Old Sheffield Plate with a chapter on Britannia Metal.* 1955.

POTTERY AND
PORCELAIN ✫

ADAM WARE. Pottery made by a family of Staffordshire potters, the earliest apparently working in Tudor times. William Adam of Tunstall copied Wedgwood's jasper ware and a hard stoneware with figures in relief on a sage green ground was another product of the Adam pottery.

AGATE WARE. This was a blending of slices of white and dark brown clays to produce an imitation of the natural stone and was known as 'solid agate'. The clouded ware, also called agate and generally classed as Whieldon ware, was a cream body coloured by oxides of copper, cobalt, manganese and others dusted on in patches before glazing, which after firing produced the variegated colours. Wedgwood who had formerly been in partnership with Whieldon later produced a shaded ware imitating the agate.

AMORNI. Italian for cupids; little figures used in ornaments.

AMSTEL. A factory for making hard paste porcelain was started at Weesp near Amsterdam, Holland in 1764; afterwards transferred, under different ownerships, to other centres and eventually to Nieuwer Amstel where it ceased to operate in 1810.

ARTIFICIAL PORCELAIN. Porcelain wares, commonly called china, are of two groups known, technically, as 'true' or hard paste and 'artificial' or soft paste, and, quoting from a booklet, *Analysed Specimens of English Porcelain* issued by the Victoria and Albert Museum, the artificial may be divided into (1) Glassy porcelains consisting of pipe-clay and a vitreous frit, lime being often added in quantity; (2) Early bone porcelains in which bone-ash was added to the glassy group; (3) Soapstone porcelains in which steatite (soapstone) was added to the glassy paste as a substitute for china clay; (4) Hybrid or modern bone porcelains in which the ingredients of hard paste—china clay and china stone—were combined with bone-ash.

ASTBURY WARE. John Astbury worked at the Elers (q.v.) factory, later (about 1710) starting for himself at Shelton, Staffordshire where he made red, black and salt-glazed ware of the type he had learned at Elers. The ware more generally associated with his name is an earthenware of different colours decorated with ornaments in pipe-clay and covered with salt-glaze. Since Astbury's time (he died in 1743) his name has come to denote the type of pottery made by him, but not necessarily made at his factory. The business was carried on by his son Thomas who produced some attractive, if rather crudely modelled, figures and copied Whieldon's agate ware. The Portobello bowl commemorating the defeat of the Spanish fleet by Admiral Vernon in 1739, now in the British Museum, is believed to have been made by John Astbury; and there is a black-ware teapot marked ASTBURY (probably Thomas) in the same Museum.

BALTIMORE, MARYLAND POTTERY. A pottery was built at Baltimore, Maryland by Edwin Bennett in 1846 who was joined two years later by his brother William, the partnership being dissolved in 1856. Among the wares made by the Bennetts were a fine earthenware, majolica, parian and artificial bone china. A modeller, Charles Coxon, employed by them produced various unusual pitchers with hound or dolphin handles and others in which he introduced the figure of a wild boar, stag hunting and similar subjects. During the partnership, the mark of the pottery was *E. & W. Bennett,*

Canton Avenue, Baltimore, Md., and after William left, it was *E.B.* Neither of these marks, however, was used on all the wares, some of which are unmarked. For a short time in the later 19th century, Bennett made Belleek ware after the style of that produced in Ireland. *See* BELLEEK.

BAT PRINTING. A method of transfer printing adopted by Flight, Barr and Flight at the Worcester porcelain factory. Instead of an ink impression on paper from a line engraving of a design being transferred to the porcelain body, the design was stippled on the plate which was carefully oiled to ensure the oil being restricted to the engraved lines. An impression was taken on to a bat (thin slab) of glue and from this transferred to the porcelain, thus leaving the 'design in oil' on the surface; the desired colour would be dusted on and so 'cling' to the oiled lines, after which the article was put in the kiln.

BELLEEK (IRELAND). A factory established in 1857 at Belleek, Co. Fermanagh, Ireland produced porcelain from china clay and felspar found in the neighbourhood. The ware is unusually thin with a lustre resembling the iridescent sheen of the inside layer of large shells. Table ware and ornaments were equally thin and lustrous, the designs for the ornaments being largely marine subjects such as dolphins, tritons, shells, etc. Colour was introduced by applied shamrock leaves of a remarkably natural green. The ware is marked with the name and a mark combining a harp, greyhound, tower and shamrock.

BELLEEK WARE (UNITED STATES). Appreciable quantities of Irish Belleek were exported to the United States during the late 19th century and some of the potteries there, after various experiments, produced a similar thin lustrous porcelain. Bennett of Baltimore made Belleek for a short time and it was produced by other factories, the most successful being the Etruria Pottery and the Lenox Pottery both of Trenton, New Jersey.

BELLARMINE. See GREYBEARD.

BERGEN, NEW JERSEY. A pottery was started in 1825 at Bergen, New Jersey by a group incorporated under the title, The Jersey Porcelain and Earthenware Company. White and yellow earthenware and hard paste porcelain were produced, but the porcelain failed to compete successfully with the imported English porcelains and the Company ceased to make it after about two years.

BERLIN. Factory started by Wegely

in 1751 produced hard-paste porcelain. Marks *W.* in underglaze blue during the Wegely period. From 1761-3 (when Gotzkowski managed the factory) a crude script G. After that, it became a royal factory and the mark was two sceptres crossed saltire; later the orb and cross or the eagle crowned

and displayed over the letters *K.P.M.* (*Konigliche Porzellan Manufactur*).

BIANCO SOPRA BIANCO. (White over white). Decoration in white over white tin enamel adopted at the Bristol delft factory.

BISCUIT. In the pottery world, biscuit is ware which has received its first firing before being glazed. The clay article is allowed to dry naturally until hard enough to be handled; it is then finished and bits such as handles and spouts are fixed on with slip (liquid clay) or, as it is called, luted. After completion, it is enclosed in a saggar (a box made of fire-clay), to protect it from the gases and flames of the fire in the kiln, and baked for several days. When it has cooled gradually, it is taken from the kiln and that is biscuit.

BISTRE. Various shades of brown made from soot of wood; often found in the decoration of German pottery.

BLACK BASALTES. Black unglazed stoneware had been made in Staffordshire long before Wedgwood's time, but it was he who developed it to the rich character that distinguishes the urns, busts, vases and his 'Etruscan' ware, painted with unglazed colours, intended as copies of the Etruscan black moulded ware believed to have been made at least twenty-five centuries ago.

BLACK POT. Coarse crockery exposed to heavy smoke while being burned in place of glazing to close the pores.

BLOCK. A proof of a decoration cast in clay from a metal mould and fired hard, from which plaster of paris moulds may be taken. Moulded forms were made by pouring fluid clay called slip into the mould which absorbs the moisture when the slip forms a skin on the walls.

BOBÊCHE. The movable nozzle with a wax pan fitted in the socket of a candlestick originally intended to catch the dripping wax.

BOSCAGE. A term used to denote the floral and foliated decoration forming a bower with figures; much favoured by the Chelsea modellers.

BONE-ASH. Residue from calcined bones of oxen. See ARTIFICIAL PORCELAIN.

BONNIN AND MORRIS. (Southwark, Philadelphia). A 'China Works' was built in the Southwark section of Philadelphia in 1769 by Gousse Bonnin and George Anthony Morris. It has been suggested that Bonnin had worked at the Bow, London, factory and in a handbill these enterprising Americans claimed they could produce porcelain equal to that made at the Bow factory. Unfortunately, they soon discovered it could not be produced at a price to compete commercially with the imported English ware; and finding the 'liquid assets' evaporating, they sought a loan from the Legislature. This was refused, however, and after unsuccessful efforts to raise funds from other sources, the factory closed after less than five years. From examples that have been attributed to this early American enterprise, the body was a soft paste of creamy tone with a clear glaze. The shapes were copied from those of Bow, Chelsea and Worcester and a favourite decoration seems to have been small flower blossoms moulded in low relief and applied. There are indications that a letter P in blue was used as a mark.

Bow. With the establishment of

the factory at Stratford-le-Bow, now in that part of London called the East End, there is the first reference to the use of bone-ash as an ingredient in making porcelain —the ingredient that gave English porcelain a distinctive character. In 1744, Edward Heyleyn and Thomas Frye were granted a patent to make porcelain of an American clay called *unaker* (imported from Virginia) and a glassy frit (probably partially fused sand or flint with potash). Four years later, however, another patent was taken out. In this the clay was not mentioned, but a new ingredient was introduced which analyses show to be bone-ash. Bow porcelain passed through a long experimental period, consequently it varies considerably. The first body or paste was glassy, often without decoration, that is, left in the white, though some of it was not particularly white; and

87

while the thin parts of the body are translucent, the thicker parts are opaque. The later body is much harder and whiter and changes occur with the glaze; the earlier glaze was quite soft and had a yellowish tint, but later the glaze was harder. A fairly generous amount of lead was used in the Bow glaze and this is shown by the iridescence similar to that seen with old glass due to the decay of the lead. Bow productions were simpler than those of its rival Chelsea. Many figures and statuettes were made at Bow, but neither the modelling nor decoration equals the more advanced technique of the Chelsea pieces. Quantities of table-ware were produced and much of this is decorated with designs borrowed from Oriental porcelains. The Bow artists seem to have had a fondness for the rich red, green, blue and gold of the Japanese Imari ware, referred to as the 'Old Japan' patterns. These were painted in overglaze enamels, i.e. the decoration was added after the biscuit had been glazed; and the Bow artists copied the Chinese blue decoration which was painted under glaze and is known as blue and white. Other patterns included a quail or partridge, a prunus branch with birds sometimes with a border of small flowers. Marks attributed to Bow are many, but not all are certain. The most generally accepted are an anchor or an anchor with a dagger. Of the others, there is a bow with an arrow; an arrow with a circle on the end of the shaft and a shaft with a cross-bar and a circle at the top

88

surmounted by a crescent (intended for a caduceus). And there are various letters and symbols used by artists and painters.

BRISTOL. Porcelain was made in

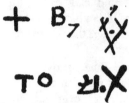

Bristol as early as about 1750 and examples still exist. In 1770, William Cookworthy transferred his Plymouth factory to Bristol where the famous hard paste or true porcelain was made. In 1773, Richard Champion, who had probably managed the Bristol works previously, bought Cookworthy's patent and carried on as the 'Bristol China Manufactory'. In 1781, the patent rights were sold to a company of Staffordshire potters. Bristol porcelain is very hard, and translucent with clear, brilliant glaze and not infrequently shows signs of spiral ribbing called 'wreathing' (q.v.). A characteristic decoration with the services is the free use of floral festoons or wreaths of green leaves or wreaths framing small cameo-like biscuit medallions. Biscuit plaques of finely modelled portraits, coats of arms or flower subjects were a specialty of the Bristol factory during Champion's time. Vases and exquisite figures were also made by Champion, the former often showing the influence of the Dresden styles; among the marks are the crossed swords copied from that of the Dresden factory;

another which was more commonly used was a simple cross in blue, occasionally with a date; and at times a numeral was added to the crossed swords and the cross.

BRISTOL DELFT. This ware was made at a number of factories in Bristol from about 1650 to the end of the 18th century. One of the more important factories started in 1743 by Joseph Flower produced a thinner and neater ware than that of most Bristol delft with a clear and brilliant glaze. Characteristics of Bristol delft are: a greenish-blue tint with the enamel; decorations in greyish-blue; a blue or purple ground with painted decorations; the use of white on tin enamel. *See* BIANCO SOPRA BIANCO.

BUEN RETIRO. The porcelain

factory established at Madrid, Spain in 1759. The workmen and models were brought from Naples (*see* CAPO DI MONTE). A wide variety of forms largely copied from those of other factories were produced at Buen Retiro of an unusually translucent soft paste. Often elaborately decorated. Figures are usually well modelled. Among the various marks used are the fleur de lis, two C's one reversed and interlaced and a crown.

CABARET. French name for small service of two cups and saucers and other pieces on a tray for serving such as early morning tea.

CAMAIEU. Decoration painted in various tones of one colour, to produce a cameo-like effect.

CAMBRIAN POTTERY. *See* SWANSEA.

CAMEO. Figures, etc., usually white, in relief applied to pottery. Some of the finest were produced by Wedgwood.

CAPO DI MONTE. Factory estab-

lished by Charles III, King of Naples, in 1736. It produced soft paste porcelain with a slight tinge varying in tone and a rich soft glaze. Characteristic decorations were modelled and applied small figures, shells and other marine subjects in relief. It is commonly thought that ware decorated with the small figures in high relief is peculiar to Capo di Monte; genuine examples are rare, many more being modern reproductions made to satisfy the demands of tourists. The Capo di Monte works were suspended when Charles III left Naples in 1759, but were restarted at Portici in 1771 and later transferred to Naples.

CASSOLETTE. A vase or box often with perforated lid to burn perfumes. *See* PASTILLE BURNER.

CASTING. *See* BLOCK.

CAUGHLEY. First pottery started at this Shropshire town about 1754 acquired by Thomas Turner 1772 who made porcelain. In 1799, the factory was bought by John Rose of Coalport Works and was active till 1814, when the Caughley works were transferred to Coalport. Turner was an engraver and is said to have originated the famous

Willow and Brosley blue dragon patterns; and quantities of Caughley porcelain were decorated with transfer prints of these in a rich underglaze blue. Other ware was decorated in enamel painting and gilding and much of this is very similar to that of Worcester. Among the several marks were arabic numerals intersected by forms suggesting Chinese characters; others were the letters C or S, a crescent in blue under glaze and SALOPIAN impressed.

CERAMIC. Term denoting objects made of clay; from the Greek *keramos*, clay.

CHANTILLY. An important French

factory established in 1725. Produced a soft paste body with a slightly creamy tone. The early glaze was opaque but later this was

replaced by a transparent glaze. The articles made show a distinct Japanese influence both in form and decoration. The principal mark of Chantilly was a hunter's horn in red or blue. The works closed in 1789.

CHARGER. A large flat serving dish.

CHELSEA. The history of this celebrated factory before about 1745 is obscure. In that year, it was managed by Charles Gouyn who in 1750 was succeeded by Nicholas Sprimont, a silversmith. Sprimont's health failing, the factory was advertised for sale in 1763, but it was not sold until 1769 when it was bought by James Cox who sold it to William Duesbury and John Heath of Derby. The Chelsea works were carried on by Duesbury until 1784 when they were transferred to Derby. The Chelsea productions vary at different

periods. Those of the early years, i.e. with the triangle mark, were a soft creamy paste and very translucent; this was followed by a thicker and less translucent body and, about 1760 bone-ash was added to the composition which resulted in a harder paste of closer texture. Some of the wares when held against the light show circular spots of particular translucency called moons (q.v.). In earlier pieces with the triangle mark the spots are minute, but those with the embossed anchor and red anchor show distinct disks or 'moons'. Similar diversity is noticeable with the glaze, that of the first period, being soft and mellow, sometimes showing tiny pinholes; during the second period it was of the same soft mellow character but more evenly distributed and, later, more brilliant and harder. The articles made at Chelsea range from table services and the well-known figures to trinkets such as snuff-bottles, patch boxes and buttons. Of the marks, the earliest, an incised triangle, is very rarely met with. The more common mark was an anchor; at first white in relief within an embossed oval, though the anchor was sometimes in red. Later the oval was omitted and the anchor, usually in gold, but occasionally in red, was used. Another very rare mark is a trident and a crown found on a few pieces. *See* DERBY.

CHIAROSCURO. Painting done with various shades of the same colour to obtain light and shade.

CHINA STONE. *See* PETUNTSE.

CHURCH GRESLEY. Porcelain made at a small factory started at Gresley Hall, Derbyshire, in 1794. Closed in 1808. Mark, *Church Gresley* impressed.

CLAY. *See* KAOLIN.

CLOBBERED. Ware painted with bright colours over the original decoration and refired. Popular about a century ago. Of little value.

CLOUDED WARES. A cream ware

coloured with metal oxides put on with a sponge which after firing became patches of green, blue, yellow and brown.

COALPORT. Factory established by

John Rose about 1790. Later he bought and absorbed the Caughley, Swansea and Nantgarw works. Principal products were table services, but ambitious vases in the manner of Dresden, Sevres and Chelsea were also made. The factory is still working. In addition to those of Caughley other marks used were COALPORT, CD, CBD and C. DALE (abbreviations of Coalbrookdale), a curious monogram of c & s (Coalport and Salopian) enclosing the letters c. s. n. (Caughley, Swansea and Nantgarw). The marks of Sèvres, Chelsea and other works, were sometimes used on Coalport copies of originals made at those factories.

COCK PIT HILL. *See* DERBY.

COLOURS. Colours used for pottery and porcelain are metal oxides which will withstand the heat of firing. They are mixed with a flux such as bismuth, borax, felspar, etc., to ensure their adhering to the surface. Some oxides withstand more heat without changing and any which will withstand the intense heat of the glost oven can be applied before an article is glazed, hence the term underglaze colours.

The larger number which require a lower temperature are applied over the glaze and are fired in a muffle kiln; these are called over-glaze and include any obtained from peroxide of iron, copper and antimoniate of lead. For gilding gold amalgam, with a flux, ground in turpentine is applied, fired in a muffle kiln and later burnished.

COMBED WARE. Ware combed or scratched with a toothed tool of leather or wire to produce a paper-marbling effect.

COPELAND. See SPODE.

COPENHAGEN. Soft paste porcelain

was made at this Danish factory in about 1760 and possibly before. The present factory was started in 1772 and its wares which are hard paste include excellent figure subjects, particularly animals, in addition to household ware. The factory was taken over by the Danish Government in 1775 and is flourishing to the present day. The mark is three wavy lines in under-glaze blue.

COSTREL. See PILGRIM BOTTLE.

COTTAGES. These ornaments were probably introduced from Holland during the early 18th century where they were used as pastille burners. They were especially popular in the first half of the 19th century when they were made of both pottery and porcelain. They then took numerous forms and were intended for various uses; toll-houses, thatched cottages, ancient churches, castle gateways and others served as models for night-light holders, money boxes, pastille burners, as well as jugs, teapots, tobacco jars, etc. Cottages vary in quality from the finely modelled and decorated examples made at the larger factories such as Worcester, Derby, Swansea, Spode, Rockingham, etc., to the rather crude productions of the less experienced potters. Some of the cottages are more or less faithful models of houses associated with some murder or other crime; these are sometimes called 'crime-pieces'.

CRACKLE. Term denoting network of fine cracks in the glaze of ware; also called crazed. Caused by a difference in the shrinking of the body and glaze when ware is removed from the kiln before it has cooled. It is a distinctive feature of some Chinese wares. The Chinese potters produced the crackle intentionally by several methods, such as adding some element to the glaze to disturb the ratio of contraction between the body and the glaze. The crackle induced by such means is quite different from the minute cracks that appear in glazes after years of use. Strictly, 'crackle' implies the intentional and 'crazed' the accidental production of the fine lines.

CROCK. A large pot or vessel of earthenware.

CROUCH WARE. An early 18th-century pottery made of a white clay found in Derbyshire. The ware sometimes has a greenish tint due to impurities in the clay.

CRUSE. An earthenware jar or pot.

DAVENPORT. A factory started at Longport near Burslem some twenty years earlier taken over by John Davenport, about 1793. Porcelain services and vases elaborately decorated after the Derby styles often with rich ground colours, were produced in large quantities until the works closed in 1882. Marks used were *Davenport*, sometimes with an anchor and *Davenport Longport*.

DELFT. Pottery covered with opaque-white tin enamel on which decoration was painted. First made in Delft, Holland in the early 17th century. Introduced by Dutch immigrant potters to Lambeth where a number of factories were started; others were established in the provinces, the most important being at Bristol and Liverpool. Dutch delft is of finer quality than the English, the body of which is noticeably coarse and the glaze often so thin that it has a reddish tinge due to the colour of the clay showing through. The Dutch painted decorations also indicate a far more advanced skill. The products were nearly all for common domestic use such as tygs, jugs, dishes, plates, candlesticks, etc.; few were of an ornamental character. *See also* BRISTOL and LIVERPOOL.

DERBY. Pottery was made at Cock Pit Hill works, near Derby before 1751, and possibly some porcelain was produced there. The Derby Porcelain Manufactory, was started by William Duesbury between 1751

and 1756. The finest Derby porcelain was made during the time of the second William Duesbury who succeeded when his father died in 1786. William the second died in 1796 and the factory was continued under the name Duesbury and Kean until 1811, when it was leased to Robert Bloor; during Bloor's period the standard of Derby porcelain declined considerably. In 1828, Bloor became insane and under the direction of the managing clerk the factory gradually failed and was closed in 1848. It would seem that the first mark was a script letter *D*; later a crown was placed above the *D* and crossed staves with six dots sometimes being added in about 1782. During the period known as Derby-Chelsea, when the two factories were under Duesbury's management (1770–84), the *D* and anchor were combined, or the anchor was crowned. Other variations were the inclusion of the monogram *D.K.* for the Duesbury and Kean period, numerals indicating numbers of models and other marks made by the potters.

In 1876, a new factory was built by the Crown Derby Porcelain Company, Limited which, in 1890, was appointed porcelain manufacturers to Queen Victoria with the right to use the royal crown as their mark and the title Royal Crown Derby Porcelain Company Limited. The mark of this later Company, which is still active has, since 1890, been *Royal Crown Derby* over the royal crown above two interlaced *D*'s.

DOCCIA. A small porcelain factory established near Florence,

Italy in 1735. It produced hard paste groups and figures and table ware. The owners bought the moulds, formerly used at Capo di Monte, from which copies of early Capo di Monte were made.

DRESDEN. The manufactory at

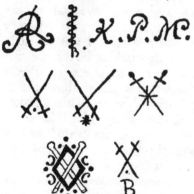

Meissen was founded in 1709 when John Böttger a chemist's apprentice of Berlin discovered the secret of making true or hard paste porcelain. Böttger became the first director and, when he died in 1719, was

followed by Johann Gregor Herold, who created the decorations in the Chinese style. During his directorship, the celebrated ground colours were introduced. Another famous man Joachim Kaendler, a sculptor who worked under Herold, was responsible for the modelling of the crinoline, harlequin and allegorical figures, animals, birds, clock cases and candelabra, many of which were mounted in ormolu. Michael-Victor Acier, a French sculptor who joined the factory in 1765, also modelled a large number of figures, but these are less robust and daintier than those of Kaendler—the well-known monkey orchestra and other series of figures are attributed to Acier. Much of the earliest Dresden porcelain was unmarked, but even by about 1724-25, a form of the well-known crossed swords was used. During about 1725-40 the cypher *A.R.* (Augustus Rex) was used, also the staff of Aesculapius. From about 1756 till 1774, a single dot was placed between the hilts of the swords, and under Marcolini's directorship (1774-1816) the dot was replaced by a star. A very early and rare mark was *K.P.M.* in script letters and this has been found with the crossed swords. *M.P.M.* (Meissner Porzellan Manufactur) was also used.

EARTHENWARE. Ware made of clay and glazed but which is distinguished from porcelain by the lack of translucency.

EGG-SHELL. Name given to the fragile, thin translucent ware made in China since about 1400.

ELERS WARE. Pottery made by two Dutchmen, John Philip and David Elers, who started a pottery at Bradwell, Staffordshire about 1690. They are said to have introduced salt-glaze to England. Well known for a fine hard red ware (generally referred to as Elers ware) with small moulded ornaments in relief. Chief products, teapots. The factory also produced a black ware not unlike the basaltes perfected later by Wedgwood.

ENAMEL. A vitreous composition applied to the glazed surface of pottery after it has been fired; used in decoration or as a ground for decoration.

EN CAMAIEU. *See* CAMAIEU.

ENCAUSTIC. Stamping red clay with a design in relief and filling the depression with white or coloured clay which is then glazed and fired.

ENGOBE. White or creamy slip (q.v.) applied as a coating to earthenware.

FAENZA. *See* MAJOLICA.

FAIENCE. Name now used to denote artistic pottery; probably derived from Faenza, Italy.

FELSPAR. *See* PETUNTSE.

FIGULINE. A piece of pottery; potters clay. *Rustiques figulines* were pottery decorated with forms of animals, plants, etc., in low relief made by a French 16th-century potter.

FIRING. Subjecting ware to the intense heat of the kiln (q.v.).

FLAGON. A vessel, often bottle shape, with spout, lid and handle for holding liquor.

FLORENCE. An ancient Italian document discovered about a century

ago, records that 'Toward the end of the sixteenth century, the princes of the House of Medici made experiments in Florence in porcelain'. This is the first porcelain made in Europe, of which any authentic record is known. It was artificial or soft paste and marked with a dome (presumably of Florence Cathedral) and the letter *F.* Also known as Medici porcelain.

FLUX. A fusible glassy substance mixed with the metallic oxides used in coloured decoration of porcelain to fuse them to the glaze.

FRANKENTHAL. This factory was

started in 1755 by Paul Hannong who, in 1759, was succeeded by his son Joseph Adam Hannong. It produced some excellent ware and that of the best period (1765-78) holds high place among German porcelain, particularly the figures and groups. The factory was active till 1795. The first mark was a crowned lion rampant sometimes with Paul Hannong's initials *P.H.* or his monogram, and later with those of his son; another mark used after 1761 was a crown over the monogram of Carl Theodore who took over the Frankenthal works in 1762.

FRIT. A semi-fused mixture of sand and fluxes used in the composition of soft paste porcelain to make it translucent.

FROG MUGS. A drinking mug which when emptied shows a pottery model of a small frog on the bottom.

FUDDLING CUP. Three or more small cups attached in such a way that the drinker was compelled to empty all of them; from *fuddle*, to intoxicate.

FULDA. One of the smaller German

porcelain factories started in 1765, under the patronage of the Prince-Bishop. It existed for fifteen years during which some outstanding hard paste services, figures and vases were produced. The marks were two F's conjoined and crowned and a simple cross.

FULHAM. John Dwight claimed, in two patents granted in 1671 and 1684, to have discovered the secret of making both 'transparent porcellane' and German stoneware. No evidence exists that porcelain was made at Fulham, but Dwight did produce stoneware indistinguishable from the German. His earlier productions were stoneware statuettes and jugs of the type known

as greybeards (q.v.). The statuettes vary in colour from white to bronze; some of the stoneware jugs had the mottled appearance known as tiger ware and examples with contemporary silver mounts are known. The factory also made brown stoneware vessels which were decorated with hunting scenes and other ornaments in relief. After Dwight's death in 1703, the works were carried on by his descendants until 1862, when they were sold. They are now controlled by a company.

FURSTENBURG. Established in about

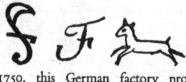

1750, this German factory progressed little until about 1770. From that time, it produced hard paste tableware and ornamental articles as well as a large number of figures and groups. The early body had a yellowish tone and there were specks in the glaze; these faults were remedied later when a white body and brilliant glaze were produced. The factory declined in the early 19th century but, in 1888, was reorganized and revived. Some of the early models were then also 'revived' and though these modern productions fall far short of the earlier standards, not a few have been sold as 'old Furstenburg'. The mark was a script F. in blue underglaze.

GALLIPOT. Small earthenware pot formerly used by druggists for ointments, etc.

GLAZE. A composition similar to glass applied to the biscuit, sealing the surface of the clay and giving the ware a brilliant coating. *See* KILN AND SALT GLAZE.

GLOST OVEN. An oven or kiln in which ware is fired to fuse the glaze; a glaze oven.

GOGLET. A long neck vessel of porous earthenware for cooling water by evaporation.

GRAFFITO. Decoration made by scratching through a covering of slip so that the colour of the clay body shows and forms the design.

GREYBEARD. Stoneware jug with a bearded mask in relief on the spout. Also called Bellarmines after the unpopular cardinal Bellarmine (1542-1621).

GRISAILLE. Style of decoration painted in varying shades of grey to produce the effect of low relief.

GUBBIO. One of the towns in Italy where majolica was made during the 15th and 16th centuries. Gubbio is especially important as the celebrated Maestro Giorgio Andreoli settled and produced his famous majolica there.

HAGUE. A hard paste porcelain

factory was active at The Hague from about 1775 to 1785. The mark was a stork holding a fish in its mouth in blue underglaze.

HARD PASTE. *See* TRUE PORCELAIN.

HEDINGHAM WARE. A pottery was established by Edward Bingham at Castle Hedingham, Essex about 1864. He produced tygs, curious jugs, vases and plaques, many being copied from early models. Bingham used small moulded applied decorations of peculiar tones of greens, blues, greys and browns; until it closed in 1905, the factory used a castle gate as its mark.

HISPANO-MORESCO. Spanish pottery with lustred decoration made during the 15th and 16th centuries. The decoration was the outcome of Moorish influence upon Spanish pottery, and parts of Arabic texts were sometimes introduced in the design. As a rule the pieces are unmarked though a mark has been found on a few.

HOCHST. The factory at this

German town succeeded, after years of experiment, in producing hard paste porcelain, in about 1740. The products later gained considerable fame from the figures, groups and medallions modelled by Johann Peter Melchior, Joseph Schneider and other noted artists employed at Hochst. The factory which was closed in 1794 used, as its mark, a wheel usually with six

G

spokes, but occasionally it has five spokes.

IRONSTONE CHINA. A fine hard pottery with certain characteristics resembling porcelain. *See* MASON.

KAOLIN. A white clay, discovered in Cornwall. *See* TRUE PORCELAIN.

KILN. A structure with a heated chamber for baking or hardening articles of clay. The unbaked ware is placed in saggars (q.v.) to protect it from the flames and gases of the fire. These saggers are stacked in the kiln and the ware fired in a high temperature for several days, and then allowed to cool gradually before it is taken from the kiln. The ware is now known as biscuit (q.v.). Later it is subjected to two further firings at decreasing temperatures, i.e. in the glost oven or glaze kiln (q.v.) to fuse the glaze and in the muffle kiln to fix the painted decoration. *See* COLOURS.

LAMBETH. *See* DELFT.

LANE END. *See* TURNER.

LEAD GLAZE. Early pottery was glazed by dusting the ware with powdered lead ore.

LEEDS. A pottery was working at Leeds long before it became prominent in 1775. Its growth was due to the well-known cream-ware made there until about 1820. This ware had a brilliant glaze of a creamy tone, but the colour was due more to the body than the glaze. A feature of Leeds ware was the delicately pierced patterns often employed with plates, fruit baskets, etc. The painted decoration is simple but good and the printed

designs are mostly in underglaze blue. The factory declined after about 1820 and from that time the quality of its products deteriorated. Marks known to have been used prior to 1820 were LEEDS POTTERY twice, arranged in a cross; HARTLEY GREEN & CO. LEEDS POTTERY in two lines and GREEN LEEDS in two lines.

LILLE. Soft paste porcelain was made at this French town for about ten years, the factory closing in about 1730. Another factory was started in 1784-85 to produce hard paste, but after some few years this was also closed. Among the marks ascribed to Lille are *à lille* in script and the letters *L* and *D* each sometimes with a cross.

LIMOGES. Hard paste porcelain was made at Limoges, but the products were restricted to household ware of no importance. The works closed in 1788.

LIVERPOOL. During the 18th century a number of potteries were active in and around Liverpool. In the earlier years of the century the chief product was delft; Liverpool delft has a noticeable bluish tone. Large quantities of cream-ware were produced by the potteries of Barnes, Chaffers and others, but records of these are few. More is known of the Herculaneum factory established in about 1795-6 and active till 1841, where earthenware, cream-ware and various other types were made. This ware is marked with the name *Herculaneum* sometimes with the liver bird (adopted from the Liverpool City Arms in about 1833).

LONGPORT. *See* DAVENPORT.

LONGTON HALL. Such information

as exists of this short-lived factory suggests that William Littler a Burslem potter experimented in making porcelain at Longton Hall in about 1752, possibly earlier; he succeeded in producing soft paste, table ware, figures, vases, etc., most of which show fire-flaws or other faults. The works ceased in 1759 and would seem to have been taken over by Duesbury of Derby. The Longton Hall mark was two crudely formed L's crossed.

LOVING CUP. Cup with two or more handles for passing from one to another.

LOWESTOFT. The first attempt to produce porcelain at Lowestoft is thought to have been inspired by the discovery (in 1756) of suitable clay in the neighbourhood. More success resulted from the establishment of a factory, some time before 1760, by a group of potters, Walker, Brown, Aldred and Richman. This firm developed considerable business and made a quantity of soft paste porcelain—their trade so increased that a warehouse was opened in London in 1770. It was formerly suggested that imported Chinese porcelain was decorated at Lowestoft, but that was proved a foolish fantasy. The paste varies from a thick opaque to quite translucent; the glaze has a distinctly blue tinge and many pieces show signs of inexperienced potting.

The factory specialized in making souvenirs, among them small circular porcelain birthday tablets, inscribed with the name of the child and the date, and little ink-pots inscribed *A Trifle from Lowestoft*. Other products were punch bowls, mugs, teapots, coffee-pots, often bearing the name of the owner and the date or *A Present from Lowestoft* in a panel framed by some simple ornament. No regular mark seems to have been used but crude imitations of those of other factories have been found on pieces made at Lowestoft.

LUDWIGSBURG. Also called Kronenberg, a German factory founded

in 1758 which made some well modelled groups and figures as well as table services. It was discontinued in 1824. The more common mark was a cypher of two C's one reversed, with or without a crown above; the cypher was replaced by T.R. in monogram in 1806 and by W.R. in 1818.

LUSTRE. Ware with lustrous metallic colours applied over the glaze and then fired. Four metals are usually employed to obtain the various lustres: Gold for gold; platinum or silver for silver; copper for copper; silver for steel; copper and sometimes gold for ruby— the ruby is also known as purple of Cassius, after a 17th-century German doctor who discovered it. The metals are finely ground with ceramic fluxes and then, usually, painted on, using suitable oils as a painting medium. Old lustres, such as Italian and Spanish were achieved by a different method. Instead of metals, oxides of the same elements were used (except gold and platinum). These were mixed with clays of a ferruginous nature (i.e. containing iron) and painted on the glazed ware. The ware was then fired to about 600° Centigrade in a reducing atmosphere (the term reducing indicating the removal of oxygen) which converted the oxide to the metal, a thin film of which formed a lustre on the glazed surface. The ferruginous clay was afterwards washed off with water. Modern lustres are usually fired in an oxidizing atmosphere, but some studio potters adopt the old method; and some also use metallic salts instead of metals or oxides. The so-called 'resist' is decorated with designs in lustre (usually silver) but on a white ground. This is done by treating the parts to remain white with some substance, such as china clay or similar refractory clay, to which the metallic solution will not adhere; in other words, it 'resists' the solution.

MAJOLICA. The generic name for pottery with opaque glaze made at various towns in Italy during the 15th and 16th centuries. The principal centres were Castel Durante,

Caffaggiolo, Faenza, Gubbio, Siena and Urbino. A large number of marks are recorded; where a piece is unmarked, it is often possible to attribute it to a particular centre by some characteristic feature in the decoration, otherwise it is virtually impossible.

MARSEILLES. Faience was made at Marseilles in the 17th century. From about 1776 until the French

$$R \quad \mathcal{FR} \quad \mathcal{JR} \quad \mathcal{R}$$

revolution (1793) hard paste porcelain was produced there. The marks used were R., F.R. in monogram, J.R. in monogram and various other potters' marks.

MASON. This factory was founded by Miles Mason in the later 18th century. The ware of his time was mostly of a Chinese character decorated in blues and reds and sometimes gilded. Later, he turned his attention to 'Ironstone China' which his son perfected and patented in 1813—to-day the well-known 'Mason's Ironstone China'. According to the patent, this excellent ware is 'Scoria or Slag of Ironstone pounded and ground in water in certain proportions with flint, Cornwall stone and clay and blue oxide of cobalt'. In addition to large quantities of household ware, a number of, often very ornate, chimney pieces and vases were made of the ironstone china and some of these still exist. The name MASON appears in all the several marks, the most familiar being *Mason's Patent Ironstone China* with a crown. This was adopted in 1813 and is used to the present day.

MAZARINE. The rich dark blue used largely at Chelsea during the red anchor period; also the old name of a plate with a deep well.

MEDICI. *See* FLORENCE.

MEISSEN. *See* DRESDEN.

MENNECY. This French factory, started in 1735, made table ware,

D.V.

ornamental articles, and some excellently modelled groups and figures in biscuit. The porcelain was soft paste with a pronounced ivory tone. The factory was moved to Bourg la Reine in 1773. The mark was *D.V.*

MILAN. Faience was made at Milan in the 18th and 19th centuries. Most of the marks include the word *Milano* in script or some abbreviation as *Mil⁰, Mil, Milᵃᵒ*.

MINTON. Founded by Thomas

Minton in 1796, this factory to-day ranks among the foremost in England. Porcelain was made by Minton's from about 1798. With their early style Minton's used gilding on a blue ground and coloured flowers in panels. During the second half of the 19th century, a number of eminent French artists were engaged as modellers and painters and many important works in the style of Sèvres were produced. The factory gained further renown

from the *pâte sur pâte* process of Marc-Louis Solon (*see* PÂTE SUR PÂTE). The earliest mark, used until 1836, suggests an imitation of the crossed L's of Sèvres with an M between; an ermine spot, generally on the copies of Sèvres models; MINTON AND BOYLE from about 1836 to 1846; and the present mark a globe with MINTON across the centre which was adopted in 1868.

MOONS. Disks of more noticeable translucency than the body due to the frit in the body not being thoroughly ground. Referred to as 'moons' they are found with Chelsea porcelain.

MUFFLE KILN. A kiln of lower temperature in which the over glaze enamel colours are fired. *See* COLOURS.

NANTGARW. A porcelain factory

NANT GARW
C.W.

Nantgarw

near Cardiff started in 1811, by William Billingsley, the famous flower painter. Nantgarw produced a soft paste brilliantly white and remarkably translucent, and a clear soft glaze. Realistic flowers in groups painted in rich colours are characteristic of this factory. Billingsley's favourite was double roses with other flowers of contrasting colours often massed in panels. In 1814, Billingsley went to Swansea, but in 1817, returned to Nantgarw and continued making porcelain there until 1819. The

factory was carried on by W.
Weston Young, for three years,
closing finally in 1822. The more
common mark was NANT-GARW
often with the letters c.w. (possibly
China Works) below, usually impressed in the paste.

NEALE. Neale & Co. was the
name of a firm at Hanley from
about 1780 to 1787, making jasper
ware and marbled vases similar to
the productions of Wedgwood.
They also made figures and household wares, some being marked
Neale & Co.

NEW HALL. This pottery near
Shelton, Staffordshire, was started
by a company of potters who
acquired the Bristol factory (q.v.)
and continued to make true or hard
paste porcelain. The paste is milk-
white with a brilliant glaze and very
translucent. The factory closed in
1825. Two marks were used: A
script letter *N.* with a pattern
number in red, and later *New Hall*
in script in thin double circles,
printed in red—the circles were
sometimes omitted.

NIDERVILLER. Faience was made at

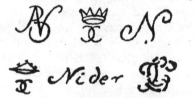

this small factory near Strasbourg
in 1760. Five years later it produced a hard paste porcelain, white
and highly translucent with a
brilliant glaze. Besides table ware
the factory produced many excellent biscuit statuettes. The

102

earliest mark was the letters B. and
N. in monogram, later ones being
two C's interlaced beneath a
coronet; a script letter *N*; NIDER-
VILLE impressed in relief; and a few
others.

NOTTINGHAM WARE. Stoneware
with a lustrous brown glaze was
made near Nottingham in the early
18th century.

NYMPHENBERG. Hard paste porcelain has been made at this Bavarian

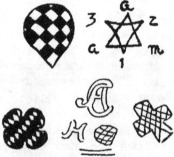

state factory from about 1747. The
paste is hard, white and dense, the
glaze clear. The factory has produced many excellent figures and
groups, among them miniature
figures. The mark generally used
was the shield of Bavaria usually
impressed; another, less common,
were two interlaced triangles known
as Solomon's Seal with figures or
letters at the points. The factory is
still active.

ORLEANS. Soft paste porcelain was

made at the Orleans factory from
1753-70 and hard paste after that
time until the factory closed in the

early 19th century. Besides the usual table ware, some figures and vases were made. The early mark was a label either in outline or solid, sometimes with the letter c or a fleur de lis below and, later, A ORLEANS and MB within a rough circular outline.

OVERGLAZE COLOURS. *See* COLOURS.

PALISSY. *See* SAINTES.

PARIAN. A ware with hard creamy white body called Parian from its resemblance to the white marble at Paros. It was discovered accidentally at the Copeland (*see* SPODE) works during experiments to recover the secret of the Derby biscuit.

PARIS. A number of minor factories were started in Paris and the outskirts during the later 18th century. Most of them produced a hard paste.

PASTE. Name given to the composition or body of which an article is made by the potter. *See* HARD PASTE and SOFT PASTE.

PASTILLE. A pastille is a small cone made of aromatic paste containing materials which burn slowly and perfume the air of a room.

PASTILLE BURNERS. *See* COTTAGES.

PÂTE SUR PÂTE. A style of decoration invented at Sèvres and developed with great success by Marc-Louis Solon at the Minton works after 1870. Figure subjects and other ornamental forms were painted in white slip on a celadon green, dark grey, black or blue porcelain ground. The slip was applied very thinly and built up by successive layers; the figure or design was sharpened with modelling tools or rounded with a wet brush. The slip being translucent, the result was remarkable gradations of tints due to the variable depth of the ground colour, the strength of which was controlled by the thickness of the slip.

PETUNTSE. A granite partially decomposed containing felspar used with kaolin in making porcelain; also called china stone. *See* TRUE PORCELAIN.

PILGRIM BOTTLE. A flask-like bottle with two loops through which a cord or strap was passed for carrying on the shoulder or the saddle.

PINXTON. A small factory started

at Pinxton, East Derbyshire about 1795, by William Billingsley, who produced a translucent glassy porcelain of particular whiteness. The wares are mostly unmarked, but occasionally a piece bears one of the several marks, i.e. a cursive *P*; the word *Pinxton*, or a crescent and star. The Pinxton works closed about 1815.

PIPKIN. A small earthen pot usually with a straight hollow handle.

PITCHER. A large earthenware vessel with open mouth, a handle (or ears) and usually a pouring lip. In Britain, generally called a jug when it has a handle; in the United States 'pitcher' is used to denote all vessels with a handle for holding and pouring liquid.

PLYMOUTH. The first factory to make hard paste in England started at Plymouth by William Cookworthy, 1768. Two years later,

the Plymouth venture was abandoned and the works transferred to Bristol (q.v.). The porcelain is very hard, white and translucent; the glaze uneven, and not infrequently marred by tiny bubbles and smoke stains. Some well-modelled figures, groups and vases, as well as table services, were produced at Plymouth. The wares made on the potter's wheel very often have spiral ridges on the sides —an imperfection known to potters as 'wreathing' from careless 'throwing' (q.v.). The usual mark of Plymouth is similar to the figure 2 with a stroke through the tail, making a combined 2 and 4 (the chemical symbol for tin) in underglaze blue, enamel colours, and on some pieces, in gold.

PORCELAIN. From the French *porcelaine*, Venus shell. The fine ware with translucent body as distinct from opaque ware known as pottery. *See* ARTIFICIAL and TRUE PORCELAIN.

POSSET POT. A large cup and cover with two, sometimes three, handles and a spout (known as the 'sucking-spout') through which the posset was sucked. Posset was hot milk curdled by some potent alcoholic addition and often spiced; at one time a popular remedy for chills and colds.

POTICHE. A round or polygonal shaped vase with small neck, rounded shoulder, nearly vertical sides and separate cover.

POT LIDS. Lids of jars or pots decorated with a landscape or design printed in colours, or black and white. Introduced about 1830 when, at first, coloured pictures printed on paper were pasted on the lids of jars containing food, and later extended to pomades. The subjects include views in London; portraits; military and naval scenes and others.

POT-POURRI JAR. Pottery or porcelain wide mouth jar with perforated cover for holding a mixture of dried sweet herbs, rose petals, lavender, etc., producing the pleasant perfume for which there are several recipes.

POTTERY. The term denoting earthenware, and other opaque ware, as distinct from porcelain which is translucent.

POWDER-BLUE. A finely powdered cobalt-blue blown through gauze over the end of a tube on to dampened ware; when glazed and fired the effect is a brilliant blue formed by the massed specks of the powdered pigment.

PRINTING. Process by which decoration is applied to ware by transfer designs of coloured ink mixed with linseed oil taken from engraved copper plates; when placed in the kiln, the oil evaporates leaving the coloured design on the surface of the article.

REFLET. Lustred or brilliant surface; used more particularly to denote the peculiar metallic brilliancy of lustred pottery, as silver reflet or copper reflet.

RESIST. *See* LUSTRE.

RIDGWAYS. Works started by Job Ridgway at Cauldon Place, Hanley in 1802. Among the specialities were lids for paste pots decorated in coloured transfer. This pottery still exists; the mark being Ridgways in different forms, usually accompanied by the name of the ware.

ROCKINGHAM. Earthenware and stoneware were made at a pottery started at Swinton, Yorkshire and

Rockingham Works.
Brameld

generally called Rockingham ware. From 1820 till it closed in 1842, the factory made good soft paste porcelain of a creamy tone with a clear brilliant glaze. The productions were table services, large ornate vases and other ornaments freely gilt. The mark was ROCK-INGHAM WORKS BRAMELD; after 1826, this was accompanied by a griffin, the crest of the Fitzwilliam family and, in 1830, the prefix ROYAL was added to the name.

RORSTRAND. Various types of earthenware and faiences were made during the 18th century at Rorstrand and other potteries in Sweden. Earlier marks were S., St. (abbreviations for Stockholm) or Stockholm in full. After the Marieberg factory was started,

Rorstrand or *Rorst* was used in place of Stockholm.

ROUEN. Faience was made at Rouen probably in the 16th century and the first porcelain to be made in France was produced at Rouen in 1673. Few pieces of Rouen porcelain (it is soft paste) are known, and none of them bears a mark. The works closed in 1696.

ST. CLOUD. As at other French

potteries, faience was made at St. Cloud many years before porcelain was produced there in 1696. The porcelain is a soft paste with a creamy tinge and the glaze is clear. Besides household ware, the factory produced vases, statuettes and other ornamental pieces. The decoration was simple and largely restricted to sprays of flowers, prunus blossoms and other floral motifs some of which were moulded in relief and applied; the pieces with moulded reliefs were often enriched with decoration in colours. The earliest marks were a sun and *StC* or *SC*; then the letter T for Trou (Henri Trou became director in 1722) was added below the *SC*—a fleur de lis has been suggested but this is doubtful. The factory was destroyed by fire in 1773 and ceased to operate.

ST. PETERSBURG. Porcelain has been

produced at this Imperial Russian factory since 1744 and an appreciable number of pieces dating from later years are in our British public museums. The customary mark was the initial of the reigning emperor or empress with the imperial crown above.

SAGGER. A fire-clay box in which ware is placed when being fired in the biscuit-kiln to protect it from the flames and gases. *See* KILN.

SAINTES. It was at this small French town during the 16th century that Bernard Palissy made the curious vases, dishes, etc., known as Palissy ware. This famous potter experimented for many years to produce the fine enamelled ware with which his name is associated. His characteristic work was decorated with fish, shells, reptiles, plants, etc., moulded in relief and applied; dishes and other flat pieces he decorated with figure subjects, also in relief, either biblical or mythological which he copied from sculpture of his time. This work has been widely imitated, but genuine specimens are light · and sharply modelled, whereas the imitations are heavy and the modelling 'podgy' and dull.

SALT-GLAZE. A method of glazing by throwing large quantities of salt into the top of the kiln; it is done by men wrapped in wet cloths when the heat is most intense and the ware inside is white hot. The salt with the silicate in the clay forms a silicate of soda and alumina which gives a coating of hard glaze. It is said that the ancient Japanese

106

potters obtained a similar glaze by throwing seaweed on to the fire of the kiln when the ware was hot.

SCEAUX-PENTHIÈVRE. Both faience

SCEAUX   SP

and porcelain were made at this small pottery near Paris which was started about 1748. The porcelain was soft paste with an ivory tinge similar to that of Mennecy (q.v.). The Sceaux factory closed at about the time of the French Revolution. The mark was an anchor with SCEAUX or the letters SP.

SÈVRES. This celebrated French porcelain factory was started in 1756 though it had its beginning in that of Vincennes (q.v.). By 1760, the Sèvres undertaking ran into difficulty and Louis XV bought it from the Company. The great period of Sèvres soft paste was from 1756 to 1769; in the latter year the making of hard paste was added. Continued experiments resulted in a perfect soft paste body, milky white and translucent; the first hard paste body had a cold glittering quality. In the early 19th century, the soft paste was discontinued and efforts were made to produce a body as hard as that of Chinese porcelain. There was some modification of this in the later years of that century and Sèvres hard paste body became pure white, translucent and resonant. The biscuit or unglazed porcelain for which Sèvres is famous was introduced in 1751, after which time the beautiful figure groups and busts modelled by famous sculptors were made in soft paste until about 1779 and later in hard paste.

by the beautiful ground colours. The earliest of these were the *jaune de jonquil, bleu de roi* and the darker *gros bleu* while later inventions included the *rose Pompadour*, partridge eye, turquoise blue, apple green, pale yellow. The political changes in France during the later 18th and early 19th centuries are reflected in the forms and decoration. From 1756 to about 1768—the greatest period—the influence of the rococo style was dominant; this was followed by the formal elegance of the Louis XVI style. Then came the austerity of the Directoire which was supplanted by the ostentatious elaboration of the Empire period with its monumental vases, etc., and lavish use of gold. The marks are of unusual interest. The interlaced L's of Vincennes (q.v.) and the year letter placed between the L's were continued by Sèvres. All the letters of the alphabet, except w, were used and when the first cycle of twenty-five years was completed in 1777, the letters were doubled. Thus 1778 was indicated by AA, 1779 by BB and so on until 1793 (PP) when the letters were discontinued and for a few years the factory used RF (*Republique Française*) usually with the word *Sèvres*. From 1792, there was a wide variety of marks—owing to the many different epochs: First Republican, 1792-1804; First Imperial, 1804-14; Second Royal, 1815-48; Second Republican 1848-51; Second Imperial 1852-72; Third Republican 1872-1904. And there are several hundreds of marks

Among the benefits derived from Vincennes were the various styles of bird and flower painting and other decoration, and, further, the Sèvres products are distinguished used by different painters and decorators employed at Sèvres which are recorded in works dealing more fully with the history of this great porcelain factory.

SHELTON. *See* NEW HALL.

SIENA. *See* MAJOLICA.

SIGILLATION. Decoration of pottery by patterns stamped in the clay.

SLIP. Clay in a creamy fluid state.

SLIP WARES. Pottery decorated with designs in slip which, generally, was run on to the ware from a spouted vessel rather similar to the method of putting an icing decoration on a cake.

SOFT PASTE. *See* ARTIFICIAL PORCELAIN.

SOLON. *See* PÂTE SUR PÂTE.

SPODE. Josiah Spode started this well-known pottery at Stoke-on-Trent in 1770. For some years only earthenware was made. Later under Josiah the second, the factory produced the porcelain known as 'bone-china', the composition of which has remained unchanged to the present time. Opinions differ both as to the actual date of its being first introduced and who discovered it, though it is generally conceded that the standard formula was decided at the Spode factory. Josiah Spode died in 1797 and was succeeded by his son, Josiah, who invented what was called felspar porcelain, the formula of which was, seemingly, lost. Another important discovery made at the factory was the fine Parian (q.v.) body which was produced in the Copeland period, the Spode busin-

108

ess having been bought in 1833, by William Taylor Copeland, whose descendants own the factory to the present day. The products over

the nearly two centuries have ranged from the willow pattern earthenware to excellent porcelain, much of which is in the style of Chelsea, Swansea and other early factories; and pieces were, and have been in recent times, decorated with painting of exotic birds in a manner fully equal to any painted by the old Chelsea artists. At one period, when under Copeland and Garrett, the factory specialized in making miniature services for dolls' houses. The factory still owns a great number of wax and lead models of parts of figures and other pieces of Chelsea and Derby origin. These were bought by W. T. Copeland when the contents of the old Derby Works were sold in 1849. The marks vary but each is almost self-explanatory. The earliest is SPODE impressed; and this impressed mark is also found with SPODE in blue. The porcelain was mostly marked with the name in colour. Others are SPODE FELSPAR PORCELAIN; SPODE'S IMPERIAL; an imitation Chinese mark with SPODE STONE CHINA; SPODE & COPELAND, a rare mark; COPELAND & GARRETT in a circle with LATE SPODE or a crown in the centre; COPELAND in a wreath and a crown above; two plain or two ornamental C's interlaced with COPELAND below; a fly with W. T. COPELAND & SONS in a ribbon below and a few others all of which include the name SPODE or COPELAND or both.

SPURS. Small clay supports, mostly tripods, used under ware while the glaze is being fired; after firing they are broken off leaving, usually three, small marks visible.

STAFFORDSHIRE POTTERY. Various types of pottery figures, groups, Toby jugs, busts, etc., most of which are unmarked and are therefore difficult to attribute to any particular maker. Occasionally the unmarked pieces show characteristics similar to those of one bearing the name of the maker, when possibly it may be ascribed to the same potter.

STONEWARE. The term generally applied to a fine earthenware which after hard firing is partially vitrified and impervious to liquid without glazing; but various kinds of stoneware are glazed.

STRASBOURG. Faience was made at

H ♯ H ℬ ℛ·

Strasbourg in about 1709 and shortly after the factory produced hard paste porcelain. Few specimens exist to-day. The marks were PH in monogram in capitals or cursive letters and Ḥ.

SUNDERLAND. A number of potteries were started near Sunderland in the later 18th century. The products which were often roughly finished were largely mugs and jugs decorated with ships and quaint verses; and sometimes a pink lustre was used. Among the names on marked pieces are PHILLIPS & CO., DAWSON, DIXON & CO. and FELL.

SWANSEA. A factory built about 1769, later renamed Cambrian Potteries, produced a kind of white earthenware, salt-glaze and cream ware. In 1802 the works were bought by L. W. Dillwyn who, in 1814, employed Billingsley to make porcelain; this was the white translucent soft paste closely resembling that of Nantgarw (q.v.). It was made at Swansea between 1814 and

1817 and was often marked NANTGARW. After Billingsley left, Dillwyn produced a somewhat harder body in which a greenish tint

is noticeable when held to the light. This is marked SWANSEA, sometimes with one or two tridents; a third type of porcelain is distinguished by an unattractive dead white glaze. In addition to the marks mentioned another BEVINGTON & CO. SWANSEA was used from 1817 until the works closed in 1824.

TERRACOTTA. Hard baked pottery used in statuary, vases and ornamental building material. Usually a brownish-red but there are other colours. Terracotta is sometimes glazed.

THROWING. A lump of clay of suitable size for the round article is placed on a horizontal disk made to revolve by a treadle, called the potter's wheel, and rounded to the desired shape by the potter's hand and fingers.

TOBY JUG. Strictly a jug in the

form of a seated figure in brightly coloured costume holding a jug; it was most probably modelled from the engraved portrait of Toby Fillpot which was doubtless inspired by Francis Fawkes' ballad 'Toby Fillpot', published in 1761.

TOFT WARE. A class of slip-ware made in Staffordshire during the second half of the 17th century; the name Toft was derived from that of the potters of the Toft family who made some of the earliest pieces and marked them with their name. Names of other men believed to have been makers of slip ware in Staffordshire, during the later 17th and earlier 18th centuries, are recorded.

TORTOISESHELL. Oxides applied to the body and carefully blended in a warm mottling to resemble the variations of tortoiseshell.

TOURNAY. A soft paste factory was

established at Tournay, Belgium in 1750, and prospered until 1850 when it was sold. The mark was two swords crossed with four small crosses, but other curious devices, probably workmen's marks, are found on some specimens, many of which are unmarked.

TRANSFER-PRINTS. *See* PRINTING.

TRANSLUCENT. Allowing light to pass but not transparent.

TRUE PORCELAIN. Also called hard paste; is made of a non-fusible china clay called kaolin (q.v.) and china stone (petuntse) which is fusible.

TUNSTALL. William Adams (see ADAMS WARE) and a number of other potters had factories at Tunstall and made earthenware, pieces of which are marked TUNSTALL POTTERIES, A. & E. KEELING, G. E. BOWERS. It was another Tunstall potter, Enoch Booth, who was the first to fire ware to the biscuit and then dip it in the glaze.

TURNER. John Turner of Lane End, Staffordshire, one of the more successful imitators of Wedgwood's jasper ware started work in 1762 and after his death in 1786 his sons carried on the pottery. The ground of his jasper is not the decided blue which distinguishes that of Wedgwood, nor are his cameos as sharply defined. Turner invented an excellent stoneware, some of which was cane-colour from a native clay. The works were closed in 1806.

TYG. A 17th-century drinking cup for posset with two or, sometimes, three handles.

UNDERGLAZE DECORATION. See COLOURS.

URBINO. See MAJOLICA.

VENICE. The history of porcelain at Venice is divided into three periods. About 1720 to 1742 when hard and soft paste were made; from 1758-63 a Dresden potter carried on a small factory of which little is known; and about 1765 a potter named Cozzi established a factory which produced some excellent white glazed figures and groups besides a wide range of useful ware. The several marks are the word VENEZIA or the abbreviations VENᴬ., VA. or an anchor sometimes with initials. The factory ceased in 1812.

VIENNA. A factory for making hard paste porcelain was established at Vienna in 1718. It became a state

enterprise in 1744 and flourished until it closed in 1864. Quantities of figures and statuettes, both biscuit and glazed, were produced besides a large number of very elaborate vases and ornaments. Previous to 1744 specimens were marked with one of different signatures and occasionally the word VIENNE and a date. After 1744 the mark was the arms of Austria.

VINCENNES. This French factory

was started in 1740 by the two brothers Dubois who left a year or two later. For a while, it was managed by one named Gravant.

In 1745, the King (Louis XV) granted it a royal concession for making porcelain and a company was formed; the privilege of using the interlaced L's (the royal cypher) mark being granted in 1753 in which year the series of date letters was started. The first three A (1753), B (1754), C (1755), indicate Vincennes, but in 1756 the works were moved to Sèvres (q.v.). The Vincennes porcelain was soft paste with a clear transparent glaze.

WEDGWOOD. This world famous firm of potters was founded by Josiah Wedgwood who, after serving his apprenticeship, in 1752 became a partner in the Cliff Bank Pottery, but withdrew in 1754 and joined Thomas Whieldon (q.v.). In 1759, the partnership with Whieldon was dissolved and Wedgwood established himself in part of Ivy House Works, Burslem, later moving to larger premises. He started the Etruria works in 1769 and during that year took Thomas Bentley into partnership. Of Wedgwood's many experiments one of the earliest was with the cream-ware which he so improved that Queen Charlotte ordered a complete dinner service; she also appointed Wedgwood, Queen's potter, and allowed the cream ware to be known as Queen's ware. This popular body varies in colour from light orange to cream and it was used for most of the table wares as well as for figures, vases and other ornaments produced by Wedgwood in his early days; the later 18th-century Queen's ware was decorated

with a pink lustre. The beautiful black basaltes (also called Egyptian black ware) Wedgwood evolved from the black unglazed stoneware that had been known for many years. Some useful articles were made, but it was used chiefly for vases, busts, cameos and intaglios. He also produced a red ware and some excellent terracotta in various colours; another body, a fine white stoneware was, for a time, used for the plinths of the vases made of the variegated ware and later for the cameos and medallions—with the variegated wares the surface imitated marble, agate or granite. Wedgwood's most important discovery was the jasper ware, a white body he perfected about 1775. Though hard enough to be polished on a wheel, it could be coloured throughout with oxides, but a less costly method of staining the surface, called 'jasper dip' was adopted. The jasper ware was almost invariably ornamented in white relief on a coloured ground, the ground, as a rule, being one of several shades of blue, sage-green, olive-green, black, yellow, pink or lilac. The celebrated Portland vase was reproduced in jasper ware after five years of attempts and failures. Porcelain was not made by Wedgwood until the early 19th century and then only for a few years— porcelain making was resumed in 1872 and has been carried on until to-day. The mark throughout has been the name WEDGWOOD except during the partnership of Wedgwood and Bentley (1769-80) when the ware was marked WEDGWOOD

& BENTLEY in a circle at times with ETRURIA; small objects such as intaglios and cameos were marked W & B. The WEDGWOOD mark in various size capital letters was adopted in the first Josiah's time and has been retained to the present day. The name ETRURIA is sometimes found with WEDGWOOD on pieces believed to date after about 1850. The marks were invariably stamped in the soft clay of all the wares except the porcelain with which the name is in red or blue over the glaze. Pieces marked WEDGWOOD & CO. have no connection with the Etruria works; they were made by a firm who used that mark and had a small factory at Ferrybridge (1796-1800).

WHEEL. *See* THROWING.

WHIELDON WARE. Thomas Whieldon was making agate ware knife handles in 1740 and later improved and extended his products to include other variegated ware; and as the early agate, clouded and tortoiseshell ware are generally unmarked they have, as it were, by 'popular consent' come to be classified as Whieldon ware. For his teapots Whieldon adopted curious shapes such as cauliflowers and melons which are noteworthy for a splendid green glaze; it seems likely this glaze was invented by Josiah Wedgwood during the time he was Whieldon's partner. *See* AGATE WARE.

WILLOW PATTERN. Credit for originating this popular design and the Brosley blue dragon has been tentatively given to more than

one 18th-century engraver. The Willow pattern is popularly supposed to picture a Chinese love romance and to have been copied from an Oriental original design. But as it was remarked some years ago, there are no Chinese examples that might pass as being the original; moreover, the Oriental potter was far too skilful and artistic to crowd a design with as many details as are assembled in the small space of the Willow pattern.

WORCESTER. Founded by a company led by Dr. Wall in 1751 the Worcester porcelain factory is the

only one in England to have remained in continuous production from the 18th century to the present time. Wall died in 1776 but the works were carried by the same manager William Davis until he died in 1783—hence what is called the 'Wall period' is dated from 1751 to 1783. At Davis' death, the concern was sold and

H

from then it changed ownership nine times. viz: Joseph and John Flight, 1783-92; Flight and Barr, 1792-1807; Barr, Flight and Barr, 1807-13; Flight, Barr and Barr, 1813-29; Barr and Barr, 1829-40; Barr and Chamberlain, 1840-7; Chamberlain and Lilly, 1848-50 (who were joined by Kerr in 1850); Kerr and Binns, 1852-62, and in 1862 the existing Royal Worcester Porcelain Co. was formed—another factory established by Thomas Grainger about 1800 continued until 1889 when it was absorbed by the present company. Robert Chamberlain who left the factory in 1783 started a rival concern in 1789; this rivalry continued until 1840 when the two works were amalgamated. The early Worcester porcelain has characteristics distinguishing it from others of its time: The body is occasionally creamy in tone and shows a greenish tint when held to the light; the glaze is smooth and even, but there is sometimes a dryness and thinness of the glaze on the foot or base— this last feature, however, is not peculiar to Worcester but is found with products of some other factories. During the Flight and Barr period (1792-1807) the paste and the glaze have a slightly grey tint. In the early years of the 19th century after experiments toward improving the body, a bone porcelain was adopted. About 1756 Robert Hancock introduced the transfer-printed decoration and some splendid impressions are found on Worcester porcelains from the line engravings of Hancock, Valen-

tine Green and other artists. These printed decorations were in black, purple and red over glaze and blue under glaze. During the Flight and Barr period a new process known as bat-printing (q.v.) was introduced. Over the two centuries, the marks on Worcester porcelain are numerous and varied, though a large proportion are probably workmen's marks. The factory marks of the Wall period were a crescent, a cursive *W*, one of several forms of Chinese seal marks, and imitations of the Dresden, Sèvres, Tournay and other European factory marks. From 1783 to 1840 the names of the several owners, are found in varying forms, viz., *Flight, Flight & Barr, Barr Flight & Barr* or *B.F.B., Flight Barr & Barr* or *F.B.B.* Chamberlain used the full name CHAMBERLAINS with the word WORCESTER and sometimes with the London address added. The later marks are K. & B. WORCESTER on a shield for Kerr and Binns and those of the Royal Worcester Porcelain Company which flourishes to the present time.

WREATHING. Spiral ridges apparent on the sides of a 'thrown' article; i.e. shaped on the potter's wheel— wreathing which results from careless 'throwing' is to be seen on some Plymouth and some Bristol porcelain.

WROTHAM. Potteries were working near Wrotham, Kent and producing slip-ware tygs (q.v.), posset cups and other domestic ware in the 17th and 18th centuries. Several specimens are in the British Museum.

ZURICH. A porcelain factory near

Z Z

Zurich was founded in 1763. The porcelain was hard paste with a greyish tint; attempts to produce soft paste seem to have failed. Table ware was the principal output, but some figures were modelled. Throughout its brief existence of about forty years, the factory mark was a German capital Z. There are some Zurich figures of *c.* 1770 in the Glaisher collection in the Fitzwilliam Museum, Cambridge.

BIBLIOGRAPHY

BEMROSE, W.: *Bow, Chelsea and Derby Porcelain.* 1898.

BRITISH MUSEUM: *A Guide to English Pottery and Porcelain.* 1923.

BURTON, W.: *History and Description of English Earthenware.* 1904.

—— *General History of Porcelain.* 1921.

CHAFFERS, W.: *Marks and Monograms on Pottery and Porcelain.* 1900.

CHURCH, SIR ARTHUR: *English Earthenware made during the 17th and 18th centuries.* 1911.

GILHESPY, F. B.: *Crown Derby Porcelain.* 1951.

GRANT, M. H.: *Makers of Black Basaltes,* 1910.

HOBSON, R. L.: *Description and History of Worcester Porcelain.* 1910.

HONEY, W. B.: *Dresden China.* 1934.

—— *Old English Porcelain.* 1948.

HURLBUTT, F.: *History of Bristol Porcelain.* 1928.

—— *Old Derby Porcelain and Its Artist Workmen.* 1928.

KING, W.: *Chelsea Porcelain.* 1922.

—— *English Porcelain Figures of the 18th Century.* 1925.

LITCHFIELD, FREDERICK: *Pottery and Porcelain.* 1925.

NANCE, MORTON: *The Pottery and Porcelain of Swansea and Nantgarw.* 1942.

SPELMAN, W. W.: *History and Description of Lowestoft.* 1905.

Snuff box

SHEFFIELD PLATE ✫

BALL FEET TO TEAPOTS. Small balls soldered to bases of teapots to act as insulators against the heat and so protect the tops of table.

BASKETS. *See* PIERCED DESIGNS.

BIGGIN. A coffee pot or jug with a long lip and a wire holding a muslin bag through which the coffee was strained. Opinions differ as to the derivation of 'biggin'. Webster says it is 'A kind of coffee pot . . . invented about 1800 by one Mr. Biggin'. But Frederick Bradbury suggests it derived from 'biggin' or 'bagging' a dialectal word for food taken between meals and that a biggin is a can holding slightly more than a pint with a deep loose lid which can be used as a saucer.

BIRMINGHAM. Fused plate was made at the Birmingham works of Mathew Boulton after about 1764; this was the only factory outside Sheffield at which fused plate was produced for nearly a quarter of a century after its discovery.

BORDERS AND EDGES. One of the problems with fused plate was to conceal the exposed copper edge of

116

an article. The early means was to solder two pieces of metal laid back to back and tin the edges. In 1785, what is known as the silver threaded edges was introduced. This was a very thin strip of silver of the exact size of the edges on which it was to be soldered and cover. Some few years later, separate ornamental mounts were stamped in thin silver; these stampings were backed, i.e. filled with a soft solder of lead and tin which allowed them to be shaped easily to the outline of any article to which they were applied. When the mounts were stamped, a narrow edging of plain silver, known as a 'fash' was left and this was skilfully laid over the edge of the article to cover the raw copper and so doing away with the necessity for soldering on the silver threaded edges. Sheffield plate articles with silver borders come under two categories; soldered on and lapped over. Where the ornamental mount is at all elaborate and is applied to a more intricately shaped outline, the edging would be soldered on separately from the mount; but a plain mount such as a thread, or a bead, would have a fash and be lapped over the edge.

BOULSOVER. Thomas Boulsover, the discoverer of plating by fusion in 1743. *See* SHEFFIELD PLATE.

BOXES. Small boxes, generally with loose lids, were made from the early years of Sheffield plate. Unlike most similar articles which are tinned, the inside of the box shows the bare copper.

BRASS. Brass was used by the Sheffield platers though only where it was invisible as, for example, the inside tubes of telescopic candlesticks and tankard bottoms.

BRIGHT CUT ENGRAVING. As with silver, bright cut engraving was adopted by the platers toward the end of the 18th century. For a time the engraving was restricted to articles plated only on one side and owing to the depth of the bright cut, it was necessary to increase the amount of silver very considerably to prevent the copper showing. *See* ENGRAVING.

BUCKLES. Buckles made by the Sheffield platers were mostly close plated (q.v.).

BURNISHING. Before being hand polished, an article was (and still is) scrubbed thoroughly with white rag dipped in Calais sand, the ornamental parts being gone over with a hair brush. It is then washed, by which time all grease has been removed and it is ready for burnishing, i.e. rubbing with a hard substance such as agate, bloodstone, steel, ivory, etc.

BUTTONS. Boulsover's first productions were buttons; fused plated metal buttons are still made as the electro plated do not give the same wear.

CANDLESTICKS. Candlesticks were among the first articles of fused plate to be made in any quantity and the various styles followed those of silver. After earlier not-too-successful attempts, by making various parts separately and soldering them together, a new method was introduced about 1765; from that time, candlesticks were made

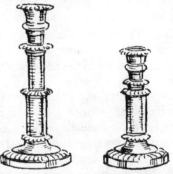

entirely from cast dies. At the opening of the 19th century, separate stamped mounts filled with lead and tin were applied and this method of ornament was used until Sheffield plate gave place to electroplating. Frederick Bradbury quotes a complete list of Sheffield plated wares made by Watson & Bradbury, and this includes upward of 1200 different patterns and types of candlesticks and branches for candelabra. A large proportion of the candlesticks were filled, which was done by putting a light rod of iron up the centre of the stem, up-ending the candlestick and pouring in molten resin, wax and pitch or similar filler.

CHASING. A form of relief ornamentation. The article is embedded in pitch which, having been made soft by heat, later hardens and holds the article firmly. The intended design is pricked on paper which is sprinkled with fine chalk and carefully rubbed to transfer the outline of the design to the article, when it is marked out by a steel tracer. The outline is 'fixed' by suitable punches which are tapped with a light hammer and the various small details similarly treated with little punches of particular delicacy.

CLOSE PLATING. This method of plating is used with such articles as forks, knife blades, cheese scoops, spurs, bits, handles, etc., and though commonly confused with, it has no relation to plating by fusion. Actually, the close plating process is quite simple. The article must be smooth and clean; and having been dipped in sal ammoniac, which is the flux, it is dipped in molten tin. A thin foil of silver is fitted on the article and pressed evenly to all parts of the metal being plated and a hot soldering iron passed over the surface to melt the tin which acts as a solder between the metal article and the silver. A hot soldering iron is then used to make the surface perfectly smooth, after which the surplus silver or fash is cut away, the edges burnished (q.v.) and the job polished.

EDGES. See BORDERS AND EDGES.

ELECTRO-PLATING. When Elking-

118

ton & Co. of Birmingham took out a patent and acquired other important patents covering electroplating, the days of fused or, as we call it, Sheffield plate were ended; for plated ware could be produced by the new process at a cost far below that of the old, and by about 1855 not one firm in Sheffield was making fused plate.

ENGRAVING. The method of engraving was to draw the design on the metal and then, using small sharp tools of various forms, cut the design out of the metal with a smooth scooping movement.

FAKES. See REPRODUCTIONS.

FORKS AND SPOONS. 'Eating tools' such as forks, spoons, ladles and the like made of Sheffield plate are relatively rare; they never reached a stage where they could compete with the solid silver ware. Various attempts were made by the platers to make them and you may still occasionally come upon trifling little tea spoons which were hammered from wire, or others where the bowls were stamped out separately and soldered to the stem, the join being visible. Forks were stamped out of fused metal lengthwise in two pieces (back and front as it were) and 'put together in two parts and filled with soft solder'. The difficulty was to avoid exposing the base metal (copper) and this was not overcome until the introduction of the electro-plating process.

FUSION-PLATING. See SHEFFIELD PLATE.

GERMAN SILVER. An alloy of copper, zinc and nickel known as

'German silver' replaced copper as the base metal for fused plating in about 1840. It is harder than copper and is now used almost entirely for good plated ware. The metal is to all intents brass with nickel added to whiten it; the name 'German silver' is explained by the first sample having been brought to Sheffield in 1830 by a German from Berlin. See PAKTONG.

INGOT. Metal cast into a convenient shape and size.

LETTING-IN. See SHIELDS FOR ENGRAVING.

MARKS. Few pieces of Sheffield plate bear the mark of the maker, though nearly all of them registered a mark under the Act of 1784. It is suggested that articles made for sale in London or other large centres, if marked, were marked with the name of the firm who retailed them rather than with that of the maker in Sheffield or Birmingham, and articles intended for sale in smaller provincial towns would be punched with a mark likely to increase their value in the mind of a potential purchaser.

MOUNTS. See BORDERS AND EDGES.

PIERCED DESIGNS. To cut the pierced work of a cake basket or other piece of fused plate with a fretsaw would obviously result in showing the copper. But the platers overcame this by an ingenious machine early in the history of Sheffield plate. The design to be pierced was drawn on the article and the piercing done by a small tool, suitable to the pattern to be pierced, fixed in the machine which was worked by hand. By careful control of a lever, the little piercing tool gradually 'squeezed' out the metal and in so doing pulled down the silver surface over the edges and covering the copper.

POTTERY MOUNTED. Various Staffordshire stoneware and other pottery jugs, mugs, etc., were mounted by the Sheffield platers with fused plate covers and rims and these are still fairly plentiful. They date mostly during the last ten years of the 18th and the early 19th centuries.

REPRODUCTIONS. The suggestion that the old process of making Sheffield plate is a 'lost art' is quite wrong. Articles can be and are made, exactly as they were long ago, of fused plate complete with silver mounts and shield. But, to-day the cost of making these fine reproductions is so high, they have to be retailed at prices at least equal to those paid for early examples. There are, however, the huge number of, usually poorly made, articles of copper covered by a thin electrically deposited coating of silver. These are more or less 'mass produced' in London and Birmingham and if we kindly include them under *Reproductions*, the unscrupulous will, by implication or by straight lying, continue to offer them to the unwary as 'Sheffield plate'.

RUBBING-IN. See SHIELDS FOR ENGRAVING.

SHEFFIELD PLATE. The romance of plating by fusion began, traditionally, in 1743, when a humble cutter,

Thomas Boulsover, repairing a silver handle of a knife discovered it had become fused to copper; there are several detailed stories of which piece of silver fused to which piece of copper, one being that Boulsover used a copper penny as a wedge and the penny being in contact with the silver handle, the two metals became joined when heated. Another later discovery of great importance was that silver and copper united by fusion would, when put through rollers, 'extend' as one metal. The possibilities were quickly realised and Boulsover's discovery laid the foundation of the craft known as Sheffield plating. An oblong ingot of copper $1\frac{1}{2}$ to $1\frac{3}{4}$ inches thick and $2\frac{1}{2}$ inches wide, of a length proportionate to the gauge and size of the sheet of plate required, was planed to ensure an even surface; it was then filed and scraped to remove any small inequalities. The sheet of silver was cut slightly smaller than the face of the copper and was also thoroughly smoothed. The two cleaned surfaces were placed together and the silver 'bedded' slightly in the copper by pressure. The silver was covered by a copper plate treated with chalk to prevent its fusing, the whole was bound with iron wire and the copper ingot and the silver were fluxed with borax at the edges where they touched. The three pieces of metal, bound together, were then put in a furnace on a coke fire and watched through a hole in the furnace door until the silver began to melt or 'weep' as it is called. This indicated that the metals were properly fused and the

ingot was lifted very carefully from the furnace, allowed to cool, thoroughly cleaned in acid and scoured, then sent to the rolling mills to be rolled into plate.

SHIELDS FOR ENGRAVING. The Sheffield plater's lot was not an easy one. He had to solve many problems which his brother, the silver-

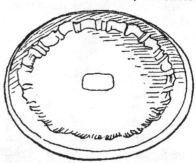

smith, did not meet with. One was to provide for the engraving of armorial bearings, monograms and inscriptions on the ware he made. To engrave on the plate would immediately expose the copper, yet it was generally customary that family plate should bear some device. During the early years after Boulsover's discovery, this engraving was provided for by the proportion of silver in the fused plate being much heavier than after the invention of the ingenious method known as soldering-in or letting-in a piece of fused plate with extra heavy silver or the still later 'rubbing-in of a silver shield', as it was called. In the letting-in process, an oval or round piece of metal was cleanly cut out of the article and this was replaced by a piece with extra heavy silver; the latter was so carefully shaped and prepared that it fitted the 'hole' exactly and, after being hard soldered, cleaned, hammered and burnished, the line of the solder was barely visible, particularly as a wavy line was engraved round the outline of the let-in piece.

'Rubbing-in of a silver shield' the later invention, was simpler. The surface which was to 'accept' the piece of silver to be engraved was hammered quite level—the rubbing-in was done before the article was shaped. A piece of pure silver was cut square or round, heated slightly and carefully flattened, the edges then being chamfered by gently hammering them on a stake (q.v.), as thin as possible. Both the plated surface and the silver shield were then rubbed with brick dust and the silver piece fastened in place by a piece of wire; it was then heated in the flame causing the two surfaces to join. The wire was removed and the piece of silver quickly burnished to ensure its being completely laid down so that no air was left under it—an analogy is the pasting and rubbing down of a photographic print on cardboard. After the silver piece was fixed, it was cleaned with acid, washed, then hammered until it was perfectly level with the surface into which it had been rubbed—actually it had been merged with the plate and thickened the silver surface. Finally, it was again burnished to ensure its being secure and free of air blisters and then hammered with a hammer covered with a piece of soft cloth. The rubbed-in silver piece will remain only slightly tarnished while the plated surface will be badly discoloured; this is explained by the fact that the rubbed-in piece is pure silver whereas the surface it has become part of, is only ·925, that is it contains a small percentage of alloy.

SILVER EDGES. *See* BORDERS AND EDGES.

SOLDERED-IN. *See* SHIELDS FOR ENGRAVING.

STAKE. A small anvil of various shapes and sizes used in metalwork.

SWAGING. A method commonly used by the Sheffield platers for shaping trays, dishes, salvers and similar articles. The swage can be likened to two jaws. The movable upper one called the jaw is shaped in various curves and grooves in cameo and the lower, called the face, is in corresponding curves and grooves intaglio. A piece of leather was fixed to the jaw to protect the silver side of the plate and the article placed between the jaws of the swage which was either struck with a hammer, or, in the case of thin metal, the jaw was pushed down by hand.

TINNING. Those parts of various articles not plated with silver were tinned by the Sheffield plate makers; for example the inside of teapots, urns, coffee pots and the bottom of pieces like trays. In the case of teapots, etc., the outside was entirely covered with glue and whiting to protect the plated surface; the pot was sprinkled with sal ammoniac and thoroughly heated and molten tin poured into the article, care being taken that the whole copper surface was coated with tin. Waiters and other smooth pieces were similarly treated. It is clear after one becomes fairly familiar with Sheffield plate that the inside and underside of pieces, made of metal plated on one side only, were invariably tinned.

Combination coffee pot and teapot with stand and lamp in Sheffield plate

BIBLIOGRAPHY

BRADBURY, FREDERICK: *History of Old Sheffield Plate.* 1912.

VEITCH, HENRY NEWTON: *Sheffield Plate. Its History, Manufacture and Art with Maker's Names and Marks.* 1908.

WATSON, B. W.: *Old Silver Platers and Their Marks.*

WENHAM, EDWARD: *Old Sheffield Plate. Its Romantic Discovery and Brief Existence.* 1955.

WYLIE, B.: *Sheffield Plate.* 1907.

SILVER ✱

AB, ABD: Mark of Aberdeen, Scotland.

ADAM STYLE. Objects of ovoid shape. Ornaments: Masks, festoons, acanthus and laurel leaves, beaded mouldings, medallions, ram's and lion's heads and other classic forms. In the United States, the classic designs were adapted to produce what may be called the Republican style. Period about 1765 to 1825.

AGNUS DEI. A lamb carrying a banner. Mark of Perth, Scotland.

ALLOY. A small proportion of copper added to the virgin metal to harden silver.

ANCHOR. Birmingham, England, town mark, left; Greenock, Scotland, right.

ANNUAL LETTER. *See* DATE LETTER.

APOSTLE SPOON. A series of spoons, each with a figure of one of the apostles with his particular emblem at the top of the stem—for example,

Andrew with the saltire cross. A complete set of 13 includes one of Christ carrying the orb and cross, known as the Master spoon. First reference, late 15th century.

ARGYLE. A gravy holder usually similar to a small teapot with an inner compartment for hot water to keep the heat in the gravy.

B, BA, BAF. Marks used by Banff, Scotland.

BACON DISH. Shallow dish with cover and wood handle fitted compartment below to hold hot water. Late 18th century.

BAYONET FASTENING. Method of fastening cover of caster to the body. Two slotted ears fixed to the cover and two notches cut on opposite sides in a grooved moulding round

123

the rim of the body. The ears on the cover pass the notches and when given a half turn, the cover engages

firmly with the body. Introduced from France in the late 17th century. Adopted by both American and English silversmiths.

BEAKER. Drinking cup derived from the ancient horn beaker. Modern glasses called tumblers are beaker shape.

BIGGIN. Name of a form of coffee percolator invented about 1800. *See* SHEFFIELD PLATE section.

BIRD. Mark used by Barnstaple, Devon.

BIRMINGHAM TOWN MARK. An anchor. *See* illustration of anchor.

BLACK-JACK. A vessel of waxed black leather with a handle, the smaller ones usually with a silver lip-band. Made in various sizes from those for drinking about 6 inches high, to those for carrying liquor, 20 inches high. 17th century.

BLEEDING BOWL. A name commonly used in England for a shallow bowl with a flat pierced

124

handle. In the United States, where they were in general use during Colonial times, a similar vessel was known as a porringer—which is far more likely to be the correct name.

BRAZIER. A pan for holding char-

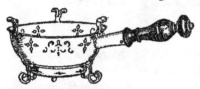

coal, with or without a turned wood handle, on three legs with brackets above. Used under a kettle, a saucepan or a dish to keep water or food hot. Few English braziers exist, but an appreciable number made by early American silversmiths have survived. Also called chafing dish.

BREAKFAST DISH. A tureen-shaped dish on feet with lid and hot water chamber for keeping food hot at table.

BRIGHT-CUT. Engraved decoration of zigzag lines popular in the late Georgian period. A revival of an Anglo-Saxon ornament.

BRITANNIA SILVER. Name applied to silver of the high standard enforced from 1697 to 1718-19 in England when a mark showing a figure of Britannia was punched on silverwork by the assay offices. This mark is still used for articles made of the high standard silver. *See* OLD STANDARD SILVER.

CADDY. A small box for holding tea. The word was originally catty from the Malay *Kati* meaning a weight of about 1½ pounds, probably the amount of tea sent in small boxes from the East.

CANDELABRUM. The name now more generally applied to a candlestick fitted with two or more branches, each to hold a candle.

CANDLE SNUFFERS. Similar to a pair of scissors, one blade fitted with a small box and the other with a plate which pinched off the charred wick and pressed it into the box—that was before the days when the burning of the wick synchronized with the disappearance of the candle.

CANN. From the Anglo-Saxon *canne* for a drinking cup. The word is obsolete in England but, in the United States, the small pear-shaped mug of the 18th century is still called a cann.

CASTER. *See* DREDGER and MUFFINEER.

CASTLE OR CASTLES. The town

Exter   *Norwich*

Newcastle
See also under Edinburgh and Cork

mark of Edinburgh, Cork, Exeter, Newcastle and Norwich. The form of castle differs in each.

CAUDLE CUP. A two-handled cup for holding caudle, at one time a popular warm drink made of wine or ale mixed with gruel or bread, sugar and spices.

CENTREPIECE. A large silver table ornament that was a modified version of the French *surtout de table*. The English centrepieces often have a large centre dish and brackets supporting smaller dishes and candle-brackets. These imposing objects were replaced, after about 1750, by a lighter style having a taller frame fitted with pierced dishes and small baskets for fruit and sweetmeats—this latter type is usually called an epergne.

CHAMBER CANDLESTICK. Portable candlestick with a tray and handle with extinguisher attached and sometimes a pair of snuffers placed through a slot in the stem of the candle-holder. Formerly used for carrying upstairs and in bedrooms before the days of gas or electric light.

CHARGER. A large dish on which the joint was carried to table; the servant who carried it was also known as the charger. Similarly the servant who carved the joint on the side table for the guests was known as the trencher; and the one who cleared the fragments left after the meal was the voider, as he scraped the leavings into a large tray or basket, known as a voider, with a large voiding knife.

CHESTER TOWN MARK. Three garbs

or wheatsheaves and a sword erect, and after 1700-1 the three lions of England impaling the three wheatsheaves. In 1779-80, the three wheatsheaves and sword was restored and has remained in use to the present day.

COASTER. A circular stand for a decanter with deep sides and a wood base covered underneath with baize; so called as it was 'coasted' along the table from one to another after the tablecloth was removed—hence the baize to prevent scratching the top of the table.

CIRCA. About. Used abbreviated to c. with a date when the exact year is unknown.

COIN. A mark used on silver during the early 19th century in some states of the United States to indicate that the metal was not of a lower standard than the silver coinage, namely, 900 parts silver in 1000.

CORK TOWN MARK. A ship in full sail; or a ship between two castles. See SHIP AND TWO CASTLES MARK.

CORNUCOPIA. Mark used by Inverness. Scotland.

CORONATION MARK. The profile of

Queen Elizabeth II crowned, in a punch of oval outline. This is a special voluntary mark, commemorating the coronation of the Queen, struck on articles of gold and silver bearing the date letters for 1952-3

126

and 1953-4, but in the latter year only to 31st December, 1953.

CORONETS, THREE. Mark used by Hull, Yorkshire.

CROSS BEARING FIVE LIONS. Mark used by York.

CROWN. Mark of Sheffield.

CRUET FRAME. A frame fitted with one large and two small silver casters and two glass cruets with silver caps is known as a Warwick cruet.

CUT-CARD WORK. Shapes cut from thin silver and applied to an article. It is similar to cutting outlines from thin cardboard. See illus., p. 128.

DATE LETTER. A letter which is part of a hall-mark indicating the year an article of gold or silver was assayed and marked at the assay office. The style of the alphabet was changed with each cycle of a fixed number of years.

see opposite page

DECANTER STAND. See COASTER.

DISH CROSS. A contrivance for

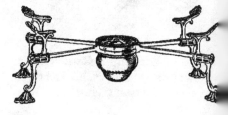

SEVEN CYCLES OF LONDON DATE LETTERS (1697-1835-6)

1716-7	1736-7	1756-7	1776-7	1796-7	1816-7
1717-8	1737-8	1757-8	1777-8	1797-8	1817-8
1718-9	1738-9	1758-9	1778-9	1798-9	1818-9
1719-20	1739-40	1759-60	1779-80	1799-1800	1819-20
1720-1	1740-1	1760-1	1780-1	1800-1	1820-1
1721-2	1741-2	1761-2	1781-2	1801-2	1821-2
1722-3	1742-3	1762-3	1782-3	1802-3	1822-3
1723-4	1743-4	1763-4	1783-4	1803-4	1823-4
1724-5	1744-5	1764-5	1784-5	1804-5	1824-5
1725-6	1745-6	1765-6	1785-6	1805-6	1825-6
1726-7	1746-7	1766-7	1786-7	1806-7	1826-7
1727-8	1747-8	1767-8	1787-8	1807-8	1827-8
1728-9	1748-9	1768-9	1788-9	1808-9	1828-9
1729-30	1749-50	1769-70	1789-90	1809-10	1829-30
1730-1	1750-1	1770-1	1790-1	1810-1	1830-1
1731-2	1751-2	1771-2	1791-2	1811-2	1831-2
1732-3	1752-3	1772-3	1792-3	1812-3	1832-3
1733-4	1753-4	1773-4	1793-4	1813-4	1833-4
1734-5	1754-5	1774-5	1794-5	1814-5	1834-5
1735-6	1755-6	1775-6	1795-6	1815-6	1835-6

EAGLE MARK. Perth, Scotland.

EASTERLINGS. Name given to Germans who were called to England by King John to improve the silver coinage; hence Sterling.

EDINBURGH TOWN MARK. A castle.

ELEPHANT MARK. An Inverness, Scotland mark.

ELG OR ELN MARK. Elgin, Scotland.

EMBOSSING. Ornament raised in relief.

ENGRAVING. See SHEFFIELD PLATE section.

EPERGNE. See CENTRE PIECE.

EWER AND BASIN. Before the introduction of table forks in the late 17th century, each guest supplied his own knife and holding his serving of meat in one hand, cut it and lifted the pieces to his mouth with his fingers. Afterwards, servants with a silver ewer, usually holding rosewater, and a deep dish or basin, went from guest to guest and poured rosewater on their hands held over the basin, drying the hands with a towel.

EXETER TOWN MARK. A Roman capital X, XON, EXON or a triple towered castle.

FEATHER EDGE. Engraved design on late 18th-century spoons and forks.

FLEUR DE LIS MARK. Lincoln town mark.

FLEUR DE LIS AND LEOPARD'S HEAD MARK. A York town mark.

It is also claimed this is a fleur de lis and half a rose. See YORK.

FOREIGN SILVER. Foreign gold and silver wares if imported by a dealer must be hall-marked on arrival by arrangement with the Customs authorities; otherwise such wares must not be removed from bond. But the Law permits a private person to import gold and silver wares without having them hall-marked on making a statutory declaration that he does not intend to sell them. If he subsequently wishes to sell them he must have them hall-marked.

Gold and silver wares sent for hall-marking which are not up to an authorized standard are to be broken by the assayers, but in the case of a foreign ware sent for hall-marking on import (or on proposed sale if imported by a private individual) the option is given to export it within a month.

Gold or silver plate manufactured abroad more than one hundred years before being imported or being sold in the United Kingdom is exempted from assay and marking. Articles of foreign plate which may be properly described as hand-chased, inlaid, bronzed or filigree work of Oriental pattern are exempt from assay and marking in the United Kingdom.

In general the law requires that any gold or silver ware ... imported and sold shall be one of the authorized standards and shall be hallmarked before sale. Some exceptions are permitted.

The above is quoted from a memorandum issued by the Worshipful Company of Goldsmiths.

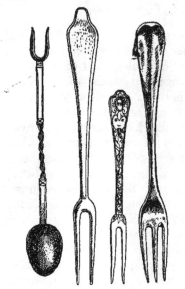

FORKS. Left to right. Sucket fork, Philadelphia, 1695. Wavy end fork, Boston, 1700. Wavy end engraved. Old English pattern, early 18th century.

FREEDOM BOX. An oval or round silver (occasionally gold) box containing the certificate presented to a

freeman by a borough. The box is usually engraved with the arms of the borough.

GLASGOW TOWN MARK. A tree with a bird on the top, a bell

hanging from a branch and a salmon with a ring in its mouth at the base of the tree or, later, across the trunk.

GOBLET. A drinking cup on a stem and foot without handles or cover.

GOLDEN FLEECE MARK. Leeds town mark.

H MARK. An early Hull town mark.

HALL-MARK. Actually the guarantee of quality. The mark established in 1300 and used by the Goldsmiths' Guild to stamp work examined and accepted at their hall.

HANAP. An old name for a large cup known as a standing cup.

HAND-WARMER. A silver sphere delicately pierced and engraved.

HARP CROWNED MARK. The Dublin standard mark.

HIBERNIA MARK. Mark adopted by the Dublin Goldsmiths' Company in 1730 to show payment of tax on silver of 6d. an ounce. See Dublin.

INCUSED. A punch or mark in intaglio, i.e. impressed in the metal.

INS MARK. An Inverness, Scotland town mark.

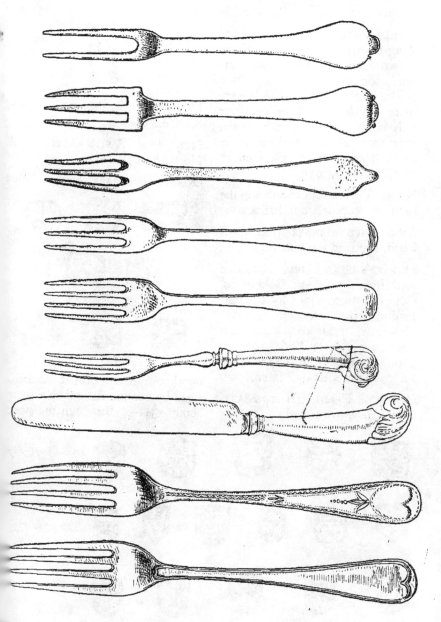

pes of 17th and 18th century forks.   1 and 2. Trifid stem.   3. Wavy-end stem.   4. Old
glish pattern, three prong.   5. Old English pattern, four prong.   6. Pistol handle fork
and knife.   7. Engraved bright-cut stem.   8. Threaded edge

JUBILEE MARK. A double profile of King George V and Queen Mary, crowned, in a punch of oval outline, commemorating the silver jubilee of their reign. A voluntary mark struck on articles of silver only bearing the date letter for the year 1933-34 and on silver wares received at the assay office up to 31st December, 1935.

KNOP. A prominent member in the stem of a cup or a candlestick.

LAMB WITH BANNER MARK. A Perth, Scotland town mark.

LEOPARD'S HEAD MARK. The mark used by the London Goldsmiths' Company since 1300; by Chester, 1719 to 1838; Exeter, 1721 to 1777; Newcastle, 1721 to 1884 when office was closed; York, 1778 to 1848. Not used from 1697 to 1718-19. *See* LION'S HEAD ERASED.

LEOPARDS' HEADS, THREE, MARK. Shrewsbury, town mark.

LILIES, POT OF, MARK. Dundee, Scotland, town mark.

LION AND CASTLE MARK. A Norwich mark.

LION PASSANT MARK. A mark show-

1598-9 to 1820-1

after 1820-1

ing that silver is of proper standard. Used by London Assay Office since about 1544-5; Birmingham, since

1598-9 to 1696-7

1719-20 to 1739

1739-40 to 1820-

from 1821-2

Examples of Leopards' Heads

1773; Chester, since 1719; Exeter, 1721 till the office closed 1882; Newcastle, 1721 till office closed 1884; Sheffield, since 1773; York, 1778 till office closed 1856.

LION RAMPANT MARK. Glasgow, Scotland, standard mark since 1819. *See* Glasgow.

LION'S HEAD ERASED MARK. Used

with figure of Britannia in a separate punch to indicate high standard silver which was compulsory from 1697 to 1718-19. Both marks are still used.

LONDON TOWN MARK. The leopard's head; crowned until 1820-1; then uncrowned. Not used from 1697 to 1718-19. *See* LION'S HEAD ERASED.

LUGGIE. A small dish with one handle (Scottish).

MARROW SCOOP OR SPOON. A spoon-like article with a spoon bowl or a long narrow bowl and channelled stem for scooping the marrow from bones. *See* p. 140.

MAZER. A maple wood bowl with silver lip band and print inside the bowl of various sizes from about 5 inches diameter and 1¼ inches deep upward. Some raised on a stem and

foot were called standing mazers. A common drinking vessel until the early 16th century; the name derives from *masa* a spot, the maple wood often being of the spotted or bird's eye variety. *See* PRINT.

MONTEIGH. A large punch bowl with deep notches in the rim, which is generally movable. Wood the antiquary, writing in 1683, says it was 'notched at the brim to let drinking glasses hang there by the foot so that the body or drinking place might hang in the water to cool them'. He adds it was 'called a "Monteigh" from a fantastical Scot called Monteigh ... who ... wore the bottom of his cloake or coate so notched'.

MOTESPOON. A large serving spoon with a strainer or 'gate' down the middle of the bowl.

MUFFINEER. A caster. Originally the name of a small caster used to sprinkle sugar, salt or spice on muffins.

MUG. Small tankard without a lid popular in silver after about 1690.

NEWCASTLE TOWN MARK. Three castles, two above one.

NORWICH TOWN MARK. A castle with lion below; a rose crowned or a rose and a crown in separate punches.

OLD STANDARD SILVER. 11 OZ. 2 dwt. of pure silver to 12 oz. Troy. *See* STERLING.

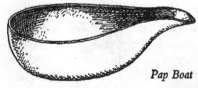

Pap Boat

133

PAP BOAT. Small shallow boat-shaped vessel with a long lip for feeding invalids.

PARCEL GILT. Partly gilt, as, for example, on the inside only.

PATCH BOX. Small box for holding the black silk patches formerly worn by fashionable beauties.

PEG TANKARD. A large tankard usually on three pomegranate feet with a vertical row of studs set at equal distances inside, the intention being that each man should drink to the next pin; 'if he drank short of the pin or beyond it, he was obliged to drink again'. Occasionally the studs are on the outside.

PIGGIN. A small pail-shaped vessel with an upright handle.

PLUME OF FEATHERS MARK. Found on silver marked at Chester.

POMANDER. A small pierced ball with interior compartments to hold rosemary, lavender and other sweet-smelling herbs, carried to counteract the unpleasant smells on the streets in olden times.

PORRINGER. Small two-handled cups, as a rule without a cover, of the 17th and early 18th centuries are referred to as porringers.

PORTCULLIS MARK. Arbroath, Scotland, town mark.

POSSET CUP. A two-handled silver or pottery cup with a spout rising close to the body called the 'sucking spout'. Posset was hot milk curdled by some potent alcoholic addition as a cure for colds and chills.

'POTATO RING'. *See* DISH RING.

PRINT. A small circular medallion embossed with some decoration; such an ornament was generally fixed to the inside of the bottom of mazer bowls (q.v.).

PYRIFORM. Having the outline of a pear.

QUAICH. A shallow drinking cup with two ears (handles) either made of staves bound with silver bands or entirely of silver engraved to suggest the staves and the bands (Scottish).

RAT-TAIL. A V-shaped tongue on the back of the bowl of some early 18th-century spoons. *See* p. 140.

REPOUSSE. Term applied to ornamention in high relief.

ROSE AND CROWN MARK. A Norwich town mark.

ROSE AND FLEUR DE LIS MARK. A York town mark. *See* p. 129.

SHEFFIELD TOWN MARK. A crown.

ROSE MARK. Montrose, Scotland town mark.

SHIP AND CASTLE MARK. Bristol town mark.

ROSEWATER DISH. *See* EWER AND BASIN.

SHIP AND TWO CASTLES MARK. Cork Town mark.

THE SALT. Until about the middle of the 17th century, the master and his guests dined with the retainers in the great hall. The master and his principal guests sat at a table raised on a dais at the end of the hall—hence the term 'high table'; other tables were at floor level. Another symbol of social status was the position of various guests in relation to The Salt. This was a very large ornamental salt holder placed on the high table in front, but slightly to the right of the master; the guest of honour was therefore as near The Salt as the host, others to his left and right being farther removed according to social rank. This explains the modern custom of placing the principal guest on the right of the host.

SKEWER. Iron skewers rather like large bodkin needles were used in the kitchen to fasten the joint on the spit and keep it in shape while turning; when the joint was sent to table the iron skewers were replaced by silver ones, some of the earlier ones being similar to a bodkin with a slot in the end.

SKILLET. A small cooking pot with a cover and handle on three legs.

Very rare in silver; surviving examples are about 5 inches diameter and date from the middle of the 17th century.

SALVER. From the Spanish *salvar*, to taste and prove food before serving—it later denoted a flat plate on which a thing was presented by a servant.

SAND-CASTER. Box with perforated top for sprinkling fine sand on the paper to dry the ink before blotting-paper came into use, about 1830.

SCONCE. A usually elaborate back plate for attaching to the wall with scroll brackets for candles.

1784-5 1785-6   1786-7 to 1819-20

1820-1   1831-2   1837-8
to 1830-1   to 1826-7   to 1889-90

SOVEREIGN'S HEAD MARK. The reigning sovereign's head was added to other marks on gold and silver from 1784-5 to 1889-90 to indicate payment of duty. *See* DUTY MARK. *Illustrations*, p. 135.

SPOONS: *see* p. 140.

SPOUT CUP. *See* POSSET CUP.

STAG MARK. Canongate, Edinburgh town mark.

STANDARD. *See* STERLING.

STANDING-CUP. A tall cup with a large bowl, some upward of 24 inches high, associated with the ancient ceremony of drinking. In early times, a large cup was passed round the company, each in turn, drinking to one or more present. The one who drank stood and held the cup with both hands and, to protect him from treacherous attack, the man next to him also stood as his pledge, showing his willingness to accept the responsibility by raising his sword while the other was drinking.

STANDISH. Former name for ink-stand.

STERLING. The standard of fineness of silver in Great Britain and Ireland. In 1300, it was fixed at 11 oz. 2 dwt. pure silver and 18 dwt. copper to 12 oz. gross (i.e. one pound, troy weight). That was in force until nearly the end of Henry VIII's reign after which the silver coinage became debased for some years and in 1559-60 the standard of 1300 was re-established and has remained 'sterling silver' to the present day. This is referred to as Old Standard and written ·925 meaning 925 parts of pure silver in 1000. The New Standard which replaced the old from 1697 to 1718-19, and is still used is 11 oz. 10 dwt. pure silver and 10 dwt. of copper to 12 oz. gross or 958·3 parts of silver in 1000. *See* EASTER-LINGS.

STERLING MARK. The word STER-LING is found on silver marked at Chester in the late 17th century; and various spellings and abbrevia-tions of it were used at Cork, Eire, during the 18th and 19th centuries.

SUCKET FORK. A 16th-century rather crude two prong fork with a spoon bowl at the other end of the stem; suckets in Elizabethan times

were plums or ginger, etc., in heavy syrup. *See* p. 130.

TAPERSTICK. A quite small candlestick to hold a miniature candle to melt sealing wax before the introduction of gummed envelopes.

TEA TABLE. In the early Georgian period, 'tea table' denoted the silver tray which held the 'tea equipage' and was supported on a mahogany stand with sockets cut in the top to take the feet of the tray and hold it firmly.

THISTLE MARK. Adopted by Edinburgh in 1759 to replace assay master's initials; and in 1914 Glasgow added it to its other marks. *See* EDINBURGH.

THREE DEMI-LIONS AND WHEATSHEAVES MARK. Chester town mark from 1700-1 to 1778-9.

TIGER WARE. Name applied to the stoneware jugs mounted in silver or silver-gilt of the later 16th century; so called for their mottled surface.

T ON TUN MARK. Taunton Town Mark.

TRAY. This word in its generally accepted sense is derived from its original meaning, namely, a long trough-like basket made of strips of wood and still called a 'trug' in country districts.

TREE, FISH AND BELL MARK. Glasgow, Scotland, town mark. *See* GLASGOW.

TREE MARK. A mark found on silver made at Greenock, Scotland.

TRENCHER. In ancient times a thick slice of coarse bread was used as a trencher or cutting slab at table. Later it was a flat square piece of wood which, in time, was replaced by the circular shape with the shallow well and narrow flat rim, the forerunner of the porcelain plate. The name trencher (from the French *trenchier*, to cut) is still used for the board on which bread is cut.

TRIPLE TOWER MARK. The town mark of both Exeter and Edinburgh has three towers, but is easily distinguishable.

TUMBLER CUP. A small bowl or wine cup about 2 inches high, with

rounded bottom, hammered so that the weight of metal in the bottom allows it to rock from side to side without overturning, whether full or empty.

VOIDER. A voider was a large tray or a basket into which the 'fragments' from a meal were collected by a servant using what was called a voiding knife—the ancestor of the tray and crumb scoop.

WAFER BOX. A small box to hold wafers or small disks of paste to fasten letters before envelopes were known.

WAX JACK. A taper holder with which a coil of flexible wax taper was wound round a horizontal spindle fitted in a frame with a tray; the end of the taper passed through a hole in a disk at the top, where it could be lighted and extinguished by a small conical extinguisher.

WHEATSHEAVES AND SWORD MARK. Chester town mark.

WINE CISTERN. Oval vessel of silver often of huge proportions which was filled with broken ice and water in which the bottles of wine were cooled. One cistern made in London for the Czar of Russia in 1734 was 5½ feet long, 3½ feet wide and weighed nearly 8,000 ounces.

WINE COOLER. A much smaller type of cistern in the form of a vase on a low foot fitted with an ice chamber. A wine cooler accommodates one bottle only.

WINE FOUNTAIN. Large upright wine container of silver fitted with handles for lifting, an ice chamber

and a tap for drawing the wine. With the cisterns, wine fountains were fashionable during the second half of the 17th and the early 18th centuries. Some of the fountains were upward of 4 feet high and weighed well over 1,200 ounces.

WRYTHEN. Twisted.

X MARK. An early Exeter town mark.

XON MARK. An early Exeter town mark.

YAWL MARK. Youghal, Eire, town mark.

YORK TOWN MARK. A half fleur de lis and half leopard's head and from 1700-1, a cross bearing five lions. *See* pp. 129 & 134.

BIBLIOGRAPHY

CRIPPS, W. J.: *Old English Plate.* 9th ed. 1906.
JACKSON, SIR C. J.: *An Illustrated History of English Plate.* 1911. 2 vols.
JONES, E. ALFRED: *Old Silver of Europe and America.* 1925.
OMAN, C. C.: *English Domestic Silver.* 1934.
WATTS, W. W.: *Old English Silver.* 1924.
WENHAM, EDWARD: *Domestic Silver of Great Britain and Ireland.* 1931.
—— *Old Silver in Modern Settings.* 1950.

The history of the assay offices of England, Scotland and Ireland and tables of hall-marks and marks used by silversmiths are to be found in
CHAFFERS, W.: *Hall-marks on Gold and Silver Plate.* 9th ed. 1905.
CRIPPS, W. J.: *Old English Plate.* 9th ed. 1906.
JACKSON, SIR C. J.: *English Goldsmiths and their Marks.* 1905.
PRIDEAUX, SIR W. S.: *Memorials of the Goldsmiths' Company.* 1896-7. 2 vols.

BOOKS RELATING TO AMERICAN SILVER

AVERY, C. LOUISE: *Early American Silver.* 1930.
BIGELOW, FRANCIS HILL: *Historic Silver of the Colonies and Its Makers.* 1917.
BURTON, E. MILBY: *South Carolina Silversmiths, 1690–1860.* 1942.
CURTIS, GEORGE MUNSON: *Early Silver of Connecticut and its Makers.* 1913.
CUTTEN, GEORGE B. and CUTTEN, MINNIE WARREN: *Utica Silversmiths.*
    1936.
ENSKO, ROBERT: *Makers of Early American Silver and Their Marks.* 1915.
ENSKO, STEPHEN G. C.: *American Silversmiths and Their Marks.* 1948.
HARRINGTON, JESSIE: *Silversmiths of Delaware.* 1939.
PHILLIPS, JOHN MARSHALL: *American Silver.* 1949.
PLEASANTS, J. H. and SILL, HOWARD: *Maryland Silversmiths, 1715–1830.*
    1930.
WENHAM, EDWARD: *The Practical Book of American Silver.* 1949.

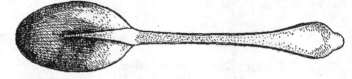

1. Wavy-end stem with rat-tail at back of bowl. 1705-6

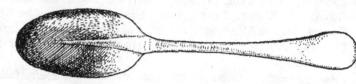

2. Round-end or Old English pattern with rat-tail at back of bowl. 1715-16

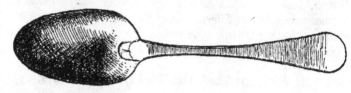

3. Old English pattern with cropped rat-tail known as 'double-drop'.
1743-4

4. Stem showing trace of former ridge with ornamented bowl. 1744-5

5. The Onslow pattern. First type of turn-down end of stem. About 1750

6. Old English pattern with turn-down end ornamented with bright-cut engraving. 1773-4

7. Old English pattern ornamented with feather-edge and showing angular projections above bowl. Late 18th century

8. Spoon bowl with channelled stem for extracting marrow from bones. 1758-9

WEAPONS, Firearms ☆

ARBALEST. A crossbow.

ARQUEBUS, HARQUEBUS OR HACK-
BUT. A portable firearm (15th-17th
centuries) for the use of infantry
and for sport, having a 'match-' or
a wheel-lock, (q.v.) Early, heavy
varieties needed a stand for firing.
Later the weapon was lightened and
designed to be fired from the chest
or shoulder. Preceded by the hand-
gun and superseded by the musket
(q.v.).

BACK-ACTION. A lock mechanism
(from *c.* 1830) used for percussion
firearms in which the mainspring
was to the rear of the cock and
tumbler. Identifiable from outside
by the hammer being at the front of
the lock-plate. Fig. I, F.

BACK-SIGHT. The sight at the
breech end of the barrel of a firearm.

BALUSTER TURN. An incised ring
turned on the outside of the barrel
of a firearm, e.g. at a barrel step
(q.v.).

BARREL LOOP. A metal loop on the
underside of a barrel through which
passes a pin or sliding bolt securing
the barrel to the stock.

BARREL STEP. The point or points at
which a barrel is stepped down in
thickness on the outside. *See*
BALUSTER TURN.

BARREL WRENCH. A spanner which
fitted round or into the muzzle of
a screw-barrel (q.v.) to screw it
off and on for loading.

BAYONET. A knife fitted to the
muzzle of a musket. The original
plug bayonet of the 17th century
was plugged into the barrel. The
socket bayonet, first used about 1700,
was fastened by a ring fitting over
the barrel. In the late 18th and early
19th century, pistols, blunderbusses
and carbines were often fitted with
spring bayonets released by a sliding
trigger guard or a separate catch at
the breech.

BELT HOOK. A long metal strip,
screwed to the side of the stock of a
pistol and parallel with it, to slip
over the waist-belt.

BENT. The notches cut in the
tumbler of a lock in which the
sear engages at the half- and full-
cock positions. Fig. II, E.

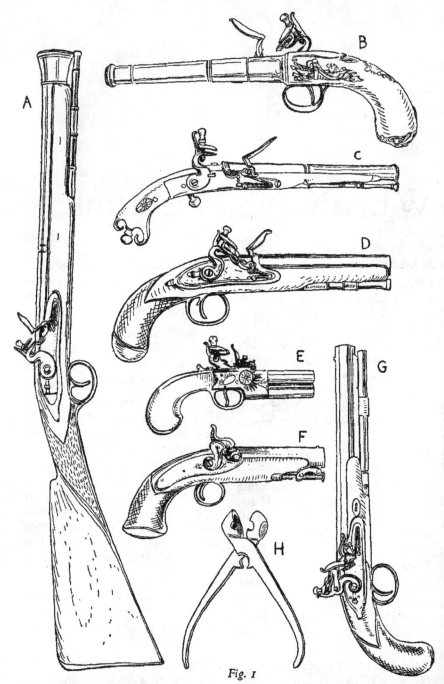

Fig. 1

A. flintlock blunderbuss. B, Mid 18th century cannon barrel pistol with silver side plate, escutcheon and butt mask. C. Scottish all steel pistol with ram's horn butt. D. Early 19th century pistol. E. Tap action under and over pistol. F. Back action percussion pistol with stirrup ramrod. G. Half stocked duelling pistol, c. 1820. H. Bullet mould

BLUING. The blue finish on metal parts.

BLUNDERBUSS. A short musket with a steel or brass barrel the bore of which is increased gradually towards the muzzle to scatter the shot. Widely used for the protection of houses and coaches in the 18th and early 19th centuries. Almost every country house had its blunderbuss over the mantlepiece. Also for naval and military purposes when they were often fitted with spring bayonets. Fig. I, A.

BORE. The diameter of the inside of the barrel of a firearm.

BOX-LOCK. A form of flint or percussion lock in which the mechanism and hammer are directly behind the breech instead of at its side. Fig. I, E.

BREECH. The rear end of the barrel of a firearm. Various systems of breech-loading, i.e. loading at the breech, were in use from the 16th century though it was not in general use until the second half of the 19th century.

BREECH PLUG. A steel plug which was screwed in to block the breech of a barrel. In later firearms it often carried a hook which hooked on to the false breech (q.v.).

BRIDLE. See Fig. II, E.

BROWNING. The brown finish on barrels and other metal parts made by a pickling process in an acid bath.

BULLET MOULD. A mould, usually of iron or brass, in which bullets were cast from lead poured in with a ladle; sometimes made to cast several bullets at once. Fig. I, H.

BUTT. The rear-end of the stock of a firearm where it rests against shoulder or chest, or, in the case of a pistol, the part held by the hand. Cf. STOCK.

BUTT-CAP. The metal mount at the extreme rear of the butt of a firearm. On pistols it was often elaborately chiselled or embossed, often in the 18th century in the shape of a grotesque mask. Fig. I, B.

BUTT TRAP. A compartment in the butt usually with a spring cover to hold caps, cleaning utensils, etc.

CALIVER. A light hand gun (q.v.).

CANNON BARREL, OR SCREW BARREL. A type of barrel fitted to pistols and blunderbusses shaped like a cannon's barrel, often unscrewing at the breech for loading. Fig. I, B, E.

CAP MAGAZINE. A small spring-loaded magazine designed to feed out percussion caps one by one.

CARBINE. A light musket or rifle with a short barrel, intended chiefly for the use of cavalry, but also used on coaches and sometimes fitted with a bayonet.

CONCEALED TRIGGER. A trigger which folded flat into a recess and was automatically lowered when the firearm was cocked. Very commonly found on pocket pistols of the early 19th century.

DAG. A short heavy wheel-lock pistol of the 17th century.

DAMASCENING. Decoration on metal applied by hammering gold or silver wire into grooves cut for it. Also used in reference to the watered patterns on Damascus barrels (q.v.).

DAMASCUS BARREL. A figured barrel formed from a mixture of iron and steel, rods of which are wound and welded together; the arrangement and spiral twisting of the rods controls the figuring which is brought up by acid etching.

DOG LOCK OR ENGLISH LOCK. An early form of English flintlock embodying a 'dog' or hook safety catch on the outside of the lock plate, which hooked into a notch in the back edge of the cock so holding it firmly in the cocked position until unhooked. This lock had a horizontal sear (q.v.).

DUCK'S FOOT PISTOL. A pistol with four barrels splayed out like the toes of a duck's foot. Also called a mob pistol which explains its purpose.

DUELLING PISTOLS may be recognized by their long (usually 10 inch or more) hexagonal barrels. During the period of their manufacture, c. 1780—c. 1825, the pistol reached mechanical perfection. Among the most famous makers of these pistols were Wogdon, Mortimer, Manton, Egg. At first full- and later half-stocked and always fitted with sights which were however only for target practice, the taking of deliberate aim not being allowed in duelling. Fig. I, G.

EPROUVETTE. A device for testing powder. It resembles a small pistol with a dial at the muzzle round which a pointer moves against a spring.

ESCUTCHEON. A metal plate set into the top of the butt just behind the barrel, intended for the crest or monogram of the owner of the weapon. In the 18th century it was often elaborate, in later, plainer weapons it became a simple shield, oval or lozenge.

ETCHING. The process of cutting a design on metal by using an acid, as opposed to engraving which is done with a tool. In etching the design is drawn with a point through a wax coating. The metal is then immersed in acid which eats into the metal where the point has removed the wax protection.

FALSE BREECH. A vertical metal plate with an oblong aperture into which the hook on the breech plug (q.v.) was hooked. The false breech was fastened to the stock by a screw through the tang attached to it.

FEATHER SPRING. The spring controlling the pan cover of a flintlock. See Fig. II, D. Also called the frizzen or pan cover spring.

FIRELOCK. An old term for a firearm having a flintlock or other spark-producing system.

FLASH-PAN. See PAN.

FLINT-LOCK. In use from the mid-17th century to c. 1840. Types are illustrated in Fig. I and parts in Fig. II.

FORE-END. The whole of the stock forward of the trigger.

FRIZZEN. See STEEL.

FRIZZEN SPRING. See FEATHER SPRING.

FULL-STOCKED. Where the stock is carried forward almost as far as the muzzle. Fig. I, D.

FURNITURE. The term usually used for the fittings or metal mounts of firearms, such as the sideplate, butt-cap, trigger-guard, escutcheon, ram-rod pipes.

FUSIL. A short flint-lock musket.

HAIR OR SET TRIGGER. A mechanism enabling a firearm to be fired with the lightest possible pressure on the trigger. In some cases there are two triggers, when pressing the rear one sets the front hair trigger. When there is a single trigger this is set by just pushing it forward. A small capstan screw near the trigger sets the tension of the mechanism.

HALF-STOCKED. Where the stock is carried forward only to about half-way along the barrel. Fig. I, G.

HAND GUN. The earliest type of hand firearm. Fired by a match applied to the touch hole, and held under the arm.

HOLLOW CURL TRIGGER. A trigger with the tip curled back in a hollow, not a solid curl, typical of the first half of the 18th century.

HOLSTER PISTOL. A long pistol such as was carried in holsters on horseback.

HORSE PISTOL. See HOLSTER PISTOL.

JAW SCREW. The long screw which clamped together the jaws of a cock so grasping flint or pyrites firmly. Fig. II, E.

LAND. See RIFLE.

LOCK. The mechanism controlling the ignition of a firearm. The igniting systems in chronological order of invention are:
 (a) The match-lock.
 (b) The wheel-lock.
 (c) The snaphaunce.
 (d) The flint-lock.
 (e) The percussion lock.

They are illustrated in fig. II, D and described under their respective names.

LOCK-PLATE. The metal main-plate of a gun lock showing at the side. It carried the firing mechanism, i.e. cock, mainspring and so on. Fig. II, D.

MAIN SPRING. The large flat spring in the lock of a firearm supplying driving power to the cock, or to the wheel in the case of a wheel-lock. Fig. II, E.

MATCH-LOCK. The earliest form of ignition system for a firearm. A smouldering match, of cord soaked in saltpetre, was applied by hand to priming powder at the touch hole. Or a pivoted arm called the serpentin holding a length of match was brought over mechanically by pulling the trigger (called the tricker) so that the burning end of the match touched off the powder in the pan. Match-locks were still in use in the East until modern times. Common on Indian, Arab and Japanese firearms. Fig. II, A.

MIQUELET LOCK. A distinctive form of Spanish lock in which the mainspring is on the outside of the lock-plate. This lock was also largely used throughout Mohamme-dan countries, e.g. N. Africa and Turkey and on Cossack pistols. Fig. II, F.

M-L. Common abbreviation for muzzle-loader.

MUSKET. A long hand firearm carried by infantry. The famous flint-lock smooth-bore Brown Bess was the standard musket of the

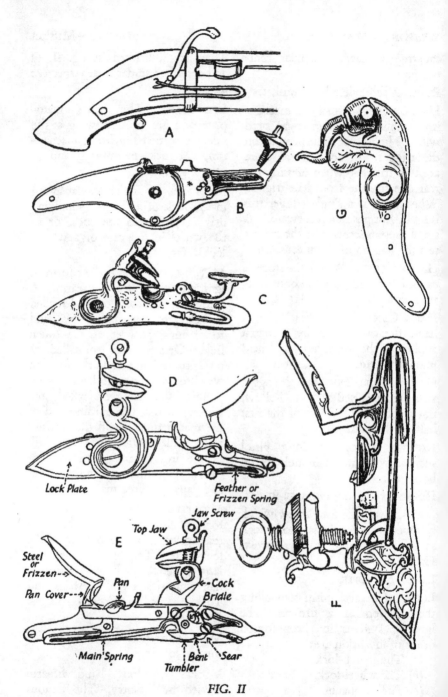

A. Match-lock.   *B.* Wheel-lock.   *C.* Snaphaunce lock.   *D. & E.* Flint-lock.
F. Miquelet lock.   *G.* Back-action Percussion lock

FIG. II

British Army from 1690 to 1840.

MUSKETOON. A blunderbuss with a long, rather narrow barrel intended to be effective at a longer range than the blunderbuss proper.

OVER-AND-UNDER. A common arrangement in a double-barrelled firearm in which one barrel is vertically above the other. Fig. I, E.

PAN OR FLASH-PAN. The small saucer-like receptacle for the priming powder beside or around the touch-hole of a muzzle-loading firearm. See RAINPROOF PAN. Fig. II, E.

PAN-COVER. The metal cover protecting the powder in the pan from damp and preventing it from falling out or blowing away before the gun was fired. In the flint-lock the pan-cover is also the steel or frizzen (q.v.). Fig. II, E.

PATRON. A box containing charges for an arquebus or musket, usually semicylindrical or rectangular, curved to the body and fitted with compartments and a hinged lid. Usually of wood or steel. 16th-17th century.

PEPPER-BOX. An early form of revolver (c. 1830–c. 1850) having its barrels—usually six—drilled out of a solid cylinder of metal.

PERCUSSION CAP. The small hollow copper cap fitting over the nipple of a percussion lock containing a fulminate which was detonated by the hammer. See CAP MAGAZINE.

PERCUSSION LOCK. A lock in which a small quantity of fulminate usually contained in a metal cap, was placed over a nipple pierced with a hole communicating with the charge in the barrel, and detonated when struck by the hammer. The percussion system was patented in 1807 by the Rev. A. Forsyth, a Scottish minister and amateur chemist. It largely superseded the flint-lock in the 1820's. Fig. II, G.

PETRONEL. A firearm mid-way in length between a pistol and an arquebus, used by cavalry, 17th century.

PIN-FIRE. The earliest efficient cartridge of modern form, invented in the mid-19th century, in which a pin, attached to the rim of the cartridge and projecting vertically above the top surface of the barrels at the break, was struck by the hammer.

PISTOL. A short firearm for use in one hand. First introduced in the 16th century and fitted in turn with wheel, snaphaunce, flint-lock and percussion action.

POWDER FLASK. A flask for carrying gunpowder for charging muzzle-loading firearms or for filling cartridges. They were made in a profusion of shapes, sizes and materials. Fig. III.

POWDER HORN. A powder flask made of horn—generally either round in section from a bull's horn or flat sided from a stag's horn. Fig. III, 6.

POWDER-TESTER. See EPROUVETTE.

PRICKER. A small bodkin for cleaning the touch-holes or nipples of guns and pistols, e.g. the pricker carried between the horns of the ram's horn butt of a Scottish Highland pistol.

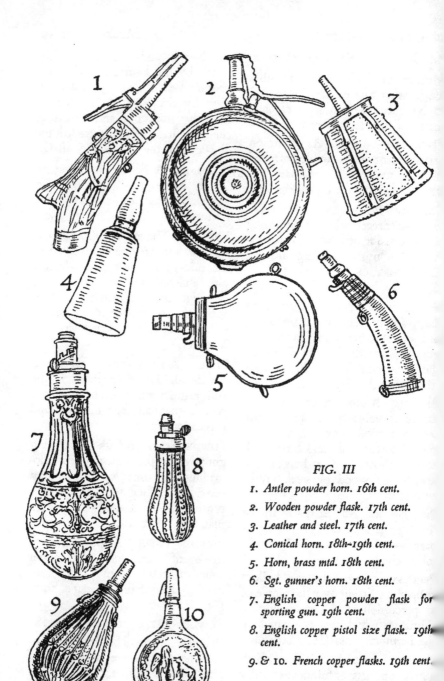

FIG. III

1. *Antler powder horn. 16th cent.*

2. *Wooden powder flask. 17th cent.*

3. *Leather and steel. 17th cent.*

4. *Conical horn. 18th–19th cent.*

5. *Horn, brass mtd. 18th cent.*

6. *Sgt. gunner's horn. 18th cent.*

7. *English copper powder flask for sporting gun. 19th cent.*

8. *English copper pistol size flask. 19th cent.*

9. & 10. *French copper flasks. 19th cent.*

PRIMER. A small flask to carry the finer powder used in the pan of a firearm.

PRODD OR STONE-BOW. A light sporting crossbow designed to shoot balls rather than quarels. Can be distinguished from the crossbow by its double cord. The prodd was used for sporting purposes up to the 19th century. It had the advantage of a silent discharge.

Liége   Birmingham   London

PROOF MARK. A proof on the barrel of a firearm to indicate that it has been tested officially in a proof house. The London, Birmingham and Liége proof marks, most usually seen, are illustrated above.

QUAREL. A form of short, square-headed bolt or arrow fired by crossbows.

RAINPROOF PAN. A late, improved form of flashpan for flint-locks in which the metal adjacent to the pan was cut away so that no water could collect around it and so spoil the priming. Fig. I, G.

RAM ROD. Rod for ramming the charge down the barrel of a firearm, usually of wood or whalebone, tipped with metal and bone, later service ramrods were of iron. The inner end of the ram rod was often fitted with a corkscrew or worm' for withdrawing the charge.

RIFLE. A gun with a rifled barrel, i.e. with spiral grooving on the inside of the barrel to give a twisting motion to the bullet and so increase accuracy. Rifling is believed to have been first used in Germany early in the 17th century. The spiral strips of the original surface of the barrel between the grooves are referred to as lands.

SAFETY CATCH. A device for quickly locking and unlocking the mechanism of a gunlock so that it may be safely kept cocked in readiness for firing. Fitted at side on lock of I, A and I, D and on top in I, E.

SCOTTISH OR HIGHLAND PISTOL. A firearm quite unlike any other produced in these islands and easily recognized. From the mid-17th century it was made entirely of metal, sometimes brass but usually steel inlaid with silver. The butt was often of the ram's horn type illustrated. The lock usually had a horizontal sear. Some of the finest Scottish pistols were made in Doune in the 18th century. Fig. I, C.

SCREW BARREL. A barrel which unscrewed at the breech for loading. See CANNON BARREL and Fig. I, B.

SEAR OR SCEAR. The catch in a gunlock which engages in the notches of the tumbler and holds the cock at half- or full-cock until, when the trigger is pressed the sear is pulled out of the notch, so releasing the tumbler and cock. Another type of sear moves *horizontally* and when cocked its toe protrudes through the lockplate to prevent the cock from moving forward. When the trigger is

149

pressed the sear is withdrawn and the cock strikes forward. Fig. II, E.

SERPENTIN. The serpent shaped moving jaw holding the match in the match-lock and the iron pyrites in the wheel-lock. Fig. II, A, B.

SHOT FLASK. A leather bag with a

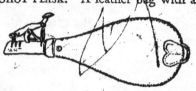

measuring nozzle, used in the 19th century for measuring shot for sporting guns. Not to be confused with a leather covered powder flask.

SIDELOCK. With the lock at the side of the breech. Cf. *boxlock* with its lock immediately behind it.

SIDE-PLATE. The plate, often engraved or pierced, on the side of the stock opposite to the lock-plate (q.v.).

SNAPHAUNCE. Successor to the wheel-lock and predecessor of the flint-lock. Made throughout the 17th century. Differs from the flintlock in that the frizzen and the pan cover are separate, in the flint-lock they are combined. The snaphaunce was especially popular in Italy. Fig. II, C.

STEEL OR FRIZZEN. The pivoted spring-controlled steel plate on which the flint in a snaphaunce or flint-lock strikes sparks to ignite the powder in the pan. Fig. II, E.

STOCK. The whole wooden part of a firearm—sometimes of brass or steel in the case of pistols—holding the mechanism and barrel. The fore part is called the fore-end and

the rear the butt. *See* FULL-STOCKED AND HALF-STOCKED.

TANG. A projection or tongue of metal. In a sword it is the narrow part at the lower end of the blade which passes through the components of the hilt and the tip of which is hammered over to hold them securely in place. In a firearm it is the projection at the breech or false breech of the barrel through which a screw passes into the stock.

TAP ACTION. A system used in flint-lock boxlock pistols with two or more barrels, whereby a lever at the side turned a cylinder which formed the bottom of the pan and in which holes were drilled communicating with each barrel in turn as the cylinder was turned, so enabling the barrels to be fired singly in rotation or all together. Fig. I, E.

TOUCHHOLE OR VENT. The small hole in the breech of a muzzle-loading firearm through which fire was communicated to the main charge in the barrel. In percussion firearms the vent is the small hole through the nipple, over which the cap was placed, and down into the barrel.

TOWER. This word, the mark of the Tower Armoury, was stamped on the lock-plates of government military firearms.

TRIGGER. The small projecting lever which, when pressed by the finger, released the firing mechanism. *See* CONCEALED TRIGGER and HAIR TRIGGER.

TRIGGER GUARD. The metal strip on the underside of the stock of a firearm curving over the trigger and protecting it from accidental release.

TUMBLER. The notched plate in the mechanism of a lock on the same spindle as the cock or hammer. As the cock is pulled back the toe of the tumbler tensions the main spring and the sear (q.v.) clicks first into the half- and then into the full-cock notches cut in the rear of the tumbler. Fig. II, E.

TURN-OVER BARRELS. An arrangement in double-barrelled firearms where the barrels were mounted one above the other and were pivoted horizontally. When one had been fired the pair of barrels could be turned so that the second was now in the firing position.

WHEEL-LOCK. An expensive and elaborate lock invented in the early 16th century and in use till the middle of the 17th. Consists of a steel wheel with its grooved rim set in the floor of the flash-pan. The wheel is revolved by a powerful spring wound up by a key that is often combined with a powder flask or measure. When ready for firing the wheel is wound up, the flash-pan lid pushed back and a piece of pyrites held in the jaws of the serpentin or cock allowed to come in contact with the rim of the wheel. On pressing the trigger the wheel revolves against the pyrites producing sparks and igniting the powder in the pan.

WEAPONS, Edged and ARMOUR ★

ARMET. A close-helmet of the XVth and XVIth centuries, especially the type illustrated in Fig. VI.

BACKPLATE. The plate of armour defending the back. It is joined to the breastplate by straps at the shoulders and sides.

BACKSWORD. A sword with the single cutting edge, the other edge being thick and squared off forming a 'back'.

BASKET HILT. A form of hilt for broadswords in which the multiple bars of a rapier hilt had coalesced in a 'basket' enclosing the hand. There were two types, first the Schiavona (q.v.), followed by the improved 'Claymore' version (q.v.).

BASSINET. A light headpiece for a suit of armour, 14th to 16th century.

BEEVOR OR BEAVOR. The fixed chinpiece of the 15th century helmet and the lower movable component of the 16th century close helmet.

BILBO. A Spanish rapier. English colloquialism for Spanish blades exported from Bilbao.

BREASTPLATE. The plate or plates protecting the front of the body, generally one main breastplate.

BROADSWORD. A type of sword, widely used in Scotland, with a straight two-edged blade, broad and flat. Usually fitted with a basket hilt.

BUCKLER. A circular shield.

BURGONET. An open helmet with a comb or combs often used in the 16th century in place of the close-helmet (q.v.), especially by light cavalry. Fig. VI, 2, 6.

CABASSET. See MORION.

CHAMFRON. The part of horse armour that protects the animal' head.

CHAPE. The metal fitting covering and protecting the point of a scabbard.

CHASING. Decorative work done with a tool on the front surface of a metal part.

CINQUEDEA. A large Italian dagger with a flat triangular blade very wide at the base and often beautifully decorated. 15th and 16th centuries.

CLAYMORE. The 'Great Sword', originally two-handed, of the Scottish Highlands. A term also, inappropriately preserved, for the Scottish basket-hilted broadsword (q.v.), which succeeded the claymore proper.

CLOSE-HELMET. A helmet entirely enclosing the head and fitted in front with a visor and beevor.

COLICHEMARDE. A form of sword-blade, often used for smallswords in which the *forte* tapers suddenly to the narrower *foible*, giving strength to the thrusting blade. The name derives from Königsmark.

COURT SWORD. A ceremonial dress sword similar in design to the smallsword but built more for decoration than use. Worn in the late 17th century, throughout the 18th and still in use in debased form. The hilt was usually richly decorated— a piece of masculine jewellery.

CUP HILT. A form of hilt of Spanish origin (17th century) in which the hand is protected by a hemispherical metal cup. Often used on rapiers. Fig. IV, D.

CUTLASS. A short backsword (q.v.) usually somewhat curved. A standard weapon in the navies of the 18th and early 19th centuries.

DAGGER. A knife usually worn at waist or hip. See CINQUEDEA, KIDNEY DAGGER, MISÉRICORDE, PONIARD, LEFT-HAND OR MAIN GAUCHE DAGGER, STILETTO.

DIRK. A Scottish dagger derived from the kidney dagger. Its sheath contains a ceremonial knife and fork, the hilt and sheath are often decorated with Celtic strap-work designs and the pommel with a cairngorm. Also a type of dagger worn by English naval officers in the 19th century.

FOIBLE. The part of a blade near the point of the sword.

FORTE. The part of a blade nearest the hilt.

FLAMBERG. A rapier with simplified hilt and slender blade introduced at the end of the 16th century. The hilt had merely quillons (q.v.), and a shallow cup guard, without *pas d'âne* or knuckle-bow. The first step in the transition from rapier to smallsword.

GORGET. The armour defending neck and throat. It was the last survivor of plate armour becoming simply a small crescent of brass worn at the neck by infantry officers until its final disappearance about 1830.

GREAVE. The plate armour protecting the leg from knee to foot.

GRIP. See Fig. IV, parts of sword.

GUARD. The part of the sword hilt which protects the hand.

HANGER. A short, slightly curved sword used by horsemen and on board ship. Also the triangular attachment by which a rapier was suspended from the belt.

HAUBERK. Shirt of mail.

HILT. See Fig. IV, A, B, D.

HOLY WATER SPRINKLER. A spiked club or mace used by clergy at war.

HUNTING SWORD. A short straight single-edged sword. The hilt is often of stagshorn with knuckle-guard, pommel and shell, of brass or silver.

KATAR. A Hindu thrusting dagger with a sharp-pointed flat triangular blade. Sometimes made with blades which divide on striking.

KIDNEY DAGGER. A dagger with quillons (q.v.) shaped like the lobes of a kidney.

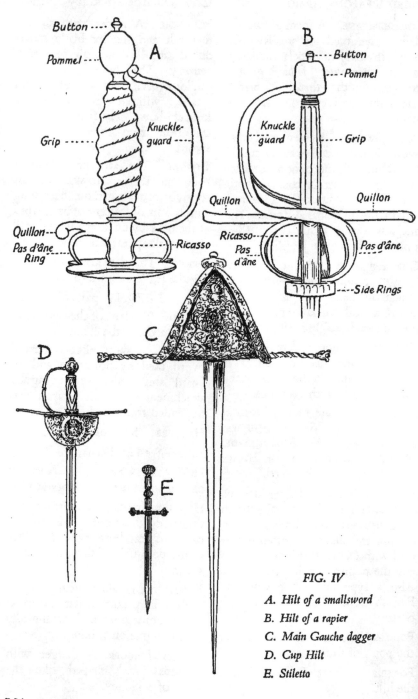

Button
Pommel
Grip
Knuckle-guard
Quillon
Pas d'âne Ring
Ricasso

A

B

Button
Pommel
Knuckle-guard
Grip
Quillon
Quillon
Ricasso
Pas d'âne
Pas d'âne
Side Rings

D

C

E

FIG. IV

A. Hilt of a smallsword
B. Hilt of a rapier
C. Main Gauche dagger
D. Cup Hilt
E. Stiletto

KNUCKLE-GUARD OR KNUCKLE-BOW. The curved bar on the hilt of a sword protecting the knuckles and curving round from the pommel to the quillons (q.v.). Fig. IV.

KRIS. A Malayan dagger having a serpentine or wavy edged blade and, usually, a handle of polished wood.

KUKRI. A large curved Gurkha knife, usually in a leather sheath on the outside of which are often pockets for two smaller knives.

LANDSKNECHT OR LANSQUENET SWORDS AND DAGGERS. Worn by the German landsknechts, foot-soldiers of the 15th-16th centuries. Characterized by a grip tapering towards the quillons.

LEFT-HAND OR MAIN GAUCHE DAGGER. A dagger held in the left hand when duelling. Often made en suite with a rapier. Fig. IV.

LOBSTER-TAILED HELMET. A modern term for the type of burgonet worn by cavalry in the 17th century, having a 'tail' of laminated plates to protect the neck. Fig. VI.

LOCKET. The metal fittings on a scabbard, e.g. that encircling its entry, from which it is suspended.

MAIL. Armour made of interlinking rings. Predecessor of plate armour. In England the age of chain mail was the 11th-13th centuries. In the East it was in use until recent times.

MISÉRICORDE. A form of narrow-bladed, sharp pointed dagger. Used to penetrate the joints of plate armour and give the *coup de grâce* to a fallen adversary.

MORION. An open helmet worn by foot soldiers of the 16th century often strengthened with a comb. The brim is crescent-shaped peaked before and behind. The Spanish morion, or *cabasset*, had a much smaller brim and no comb. A morion without a comb but with a small stalk on top is often referred to as a *peaked morion*. See Fig. VI.

MORNING STAR. Popular name for a spiked ball tied by a chain to a short wooden staff. A war flail.

PAS D'ÂNE. The two semicircular guards in the hilt of a sword which, springing from the centre of the quillons (q.v.), curve along the edges of the sword towards its point. Fig. IV.

PAULDRON. Plate armour for the protection of the shoulders.

POMMEL. *See* Fig. IV, parts of sword hilt.

PONIARD. A dagger with a short narrow blade.

QUILLONS. The cross-bar between the hilt and blade of a sword or dagger. *See* Fig. IV.

RAPIER. A straight sword with a long thin blade designed chiefly for thrusting and used especially in the 16th and 17th centuries when it was succeeded by the smallsword. Duellists used the rapier and main gauche or left-hand dagger, two rapiers, rapier and cloak, or the rapier alone. There were an almost infinite variety of rapier guards based on principles that changed with the science of fencing. *See* FLAMBERG AND CUP HILT, *also* Fig. IV.

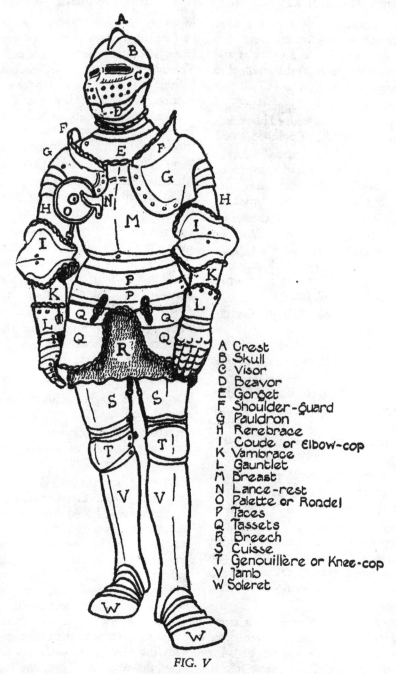

A Crest
B Skull
C Visor
D Beavor
E Gorget
F Shoulder-guard
G Pauldron
H Rerebrace
I Coude or Elbow-cop
K Vambrace
L Gauntlet
M Breast
N Lance-rest
O Palette or Rondel
P Taces
Q Tassets
R Breech
S Cuisse
T Genouillère or Knee-cop
V Jamb
W Soleret

FIG. V

RICASSO. The portion of the blade enclosed by the *pas d'âne*.

SABRE. The curved cavalry sword of Western Europe and the U.S.A. See SCIMITAR from which it is probably derived.

SALADE OR SALLET. A light open helmet of the 15th century. Fig. VI.

SCABBARD. The sheath of a sword.

SCHIAVONA. A broadsword of Venetian origin with a basket hilt, originally the weapon of the bodyguard of the Doges. The first of the basket-hilted broadswords. Generally used by horsemen but also as broadswords on foot. Cf. BROADSWORD, CLAYMORE.

SCIMITAR. The cavalry sword with a curved blade used by the cavalry of Mahommedan countries.

SHELL GUARD. Shell-shaped or oval plates, projecting from the quillons of a sword or rapier.

SMALLSWORD. Succeeded the rapier at the end of the 17th century. Designed essentially for thrusting it was used in duelling and fencing. Often had a collichemarde blade (q.v.).

SOLERET. Plate armour fitting over the foot.

STILETTO. An all-steel dagger with a very narrow blade of square or triangular section and straight quillons. Many were made in Italy.

SWEPT HILT. A modern term for a rapier hilt in which the knuckle guard joins the *pas d'âne* in a sweeping 'S' curve.

SWORD. The development of the sword since 1500 can be divided into four periods.
(1) the first half of the 16th century was that of the sword as opposed to the rapier.
(2) The era of the rapier, 1550-1625, during which the blade became longer and more slender and the guards of the hilt more complicated.
(3) A transition period, 1625-75, in which the rapier became more simple and changing towards the smallsword.
(4) The era of the smallsword, 1675 to the French revolution.
It is usual in describing a sword to refer to its point as the highest, and pommel as the lowest point.

SWORD-BREAKER. A dagger held in the left hand with deep slits cut in it to catch and break the opponent's blade, or term for the slits cut for this purpose in any dagger.

TANG. See *under* FIREARMS.

TARGE OR TARGET. A circular shield or buckler.

TASSET. Part of a suit of armour designed to protect the upper part of the thighs.

TULWAR. A curved Indian fighting sabre with a mushroom shaped pommel.

VAMBRACE. Armour for the protection of the lower arm.

VAMPLATE. Circular plate on a lance to protect the hand.

VISOR. Defence for the eyes in a helmet, often pivoted so that it may

FIG. VI

1. *Salade with visor and beavor, 15th cent.*

2. *Burgonet, 16th cent.*

3. *Morion, with comb, 16th cent.*

4. *Cabasset, 16th cent.*

5. *Armet (A, Ventail, and B, Vue, which together make the Visor; the Skull C; and the Beavor, D).*

6. *Burgonet*

7. *Lobster-tailed Pot helmet, 17th cent.*

Reproduced from *Armour & Weapons* by Charles ffoulkes by kind permission of The Clarendon Press

be raised and pierced with 'sights'.
Cf. BEEVOR.

WOLF MARK. The 'running wolf'

stamped on sword blades was the mark of the armourers of Solingen and Passau in Germany. Their fine blades made in large numbers were esteemed in all countries.

YATAGHAN. A slightly curved Balkan or Turkish sabre without quillons. Often elaborately decorated with silver, brass, coral, etc.

CPSIA information can be obtained
at www.ICGtesting.com
Printed in the USA
BVHW041712181122
652290BV00015B/76

9 781408 631553